# Credits

**Footprint credits**
**Editor**: Stephanie Rebello
**Production and layout**: Emma Bryers
**Maps**: Kevin Feeney
**Cover**: Pepi Bluck

**Publisher**: Patrick Dawson
**Managing Editor**: Felicity Laughton
**Advertising**: Elizabeth Taylor
**Sales and marketing**: Kirsty Holmes

**Photography credits**
**Front cover**: paradoks_blizanaca/
Shutterstock.com
**Back cover**: Zbynek Jirousek/
Shutterstock.com

Printed in Great Britain by CPI Antony Rowe,
Chippenham, Wiltshire

Every effort has been made to ensure that
the facts in this guidebook are accurate.
However, travellers should still obtain advice
from consulates, airlines, etc, about travel
and visa requirements before travelling.
The authors and publishers cannot accept
responsibility for any loss, injury or
inconvenience however caused.

**Publishing information**
Footprint *Focus Dubrovnik & Dalmatian Coast*
1st edition
© Footprint Handbooks Ltd
March 2013

ISBN: 978 1 909268 13 5
CIP DATA: A catalogue record for this book
is available from the British Library

® Footprint Handbooks and the Footprint
mark are a registered trademark of
Footprint Handbooks Ltd

Published by Footprint
6 Riverside Court
Lower Bristol Road
Bath BA2 3DZ, UK
T +44 (0)1225 469141
F +44 (0)1225 469461
footprinttravelguides.com

Distributed in the USA by Globe Pequot
Press, Guilford, Connecticut

The content of Footprint *Focus Dubrovnik &
Dalmatian Coast* has been taken directly
from Footprint's *Croatia* guide, which was
researched and written by Jane Foster.

# Contents

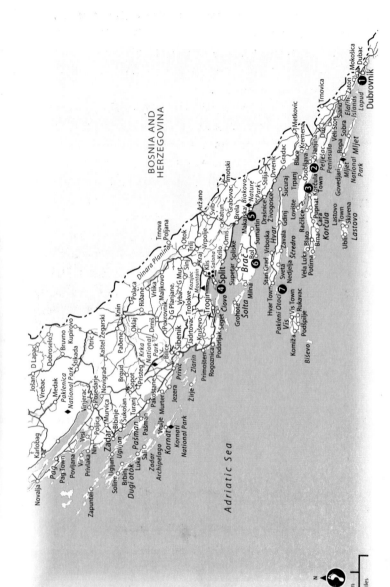

South Dalmatia, a long, thin, coastal strip backed by the dramatic Dinaric Alps, centres on the former city-republic of Dubrovnik. Contained within medieval walls, overlooking the sea, it's a magnificent complex of aristocratic 17th-century town houses, Baroque churches and paved alleys.

From Dubrovnik's Gruž port, you have regular boat connections to nearby islands. Pine-covered Mljet deserves more time than the usual day-trip. The region's most visited island, Korčula, has medieval walled Korčula Town renowned for its fine cathedral and performances of the Moreška sword dance. Korčula can be reached by car, driving along the mountainous Pelješac Peninsula, notable for its vineyards, then taking a short ferry ride from Orebić. Last but not least, remote unspoilt Lastovo, served by ferry from Split.

Central Dalmatia is home to several of Croatia's most beautiful coastal towns and islands. The main city, Split, dates back to Roman times. The nearest island is Brač, home to Bol and the stunning Zlatni Rat beach, which lies in the shadow of Vidova Gora. For many people the most beautiful island is Hvar. Venetian-era Hvar Town is Croatia's hippest island destination – the rest of the island falls away into a wilderness of lavender fields and vineyards. Further out to sea, Vis is Croatia's most distant inhabited island, much-loved by yachters.

Back on the mainland north of Split lies Šibenik, with its magnificent cathedral and the nearby Krka National Park, with its dramatic waterfalls. South of Split, the Makarska Rivijera offers pebble beaches backed by the imposing heights of Mount Biokovo.

North Dalmatia centres on the port city of Zadar, noted for its splendid Romanesque churches. From here you can drive to the island of Pag, linked to the mainland by a bridge, renowned for its delicious sheep's cheese. Further out to sea lies Kornati National Park, a unique seascape of almost 90 scattered islands and islets. Dry, rocky and practically devoid of vegetation, the islands are uninhabited. They're best explored by private yacht, but failing that you can visit them on an organized day trip.

# Planning your trip

## Best time to visit Dubrovnik and the Dalmatian Coast

Peak season in Dalmatia runs July through August, when all the region's hotels, restaurants and other tourist facilities, such as water sports clubs, are up and running. Nightlife is buzzing, with various cultural events – the top ones being the Summer Festivals in Dubrovnik and Split – and open-air bars and dance clubs along the coast. On the downside, beaches are crowded, and restaurants and bars so busy you may have to queue for a table. Accommodation prices rise steeply during this period, and availability may be scarce, so you should really book in advance.

Mid-season (May to June and September to October) is probably the most rewarding time to visit. Throughout June and September the sea is warm enough to swim (hardier types will also manage in May and October) and the beaches reasonably peaceful. Hotels and restaurants are open but not overly busy, so you'll get more personalized service. As temperatures are not unbearably hot, spring and autumn are also ideal periods for active land sports such as hiking and biking.

During low season, November to April, many hotels on the islands close down completely. Although you can't be guaranteed good weather, if you do visit Dalmatia during this period you can be almost certain there will be few foreigners around.

## Places to visit in Dubrovnik and the Dalmatian Coast

### Dubrovnik and South Dalmatia
South Dalmatia is home to Croatia's most expensive destination, the glorious medieval walled city of Dubrovnik. Dubrovnik's attractions, including the city walls, the Rector's Palace, the Franciscan Monastery and Maritime Museum, can easily absorb two or three days of sightseeing. Outside the old town, most of the modern hotels are located on Lapad Peninsula close to Gruž port, which sees regular ferries running back and forth to the tiny Elafiti islands and Mljet. The car-free Elafiti islands can be visited as day trips, while Mljet, home to Mljet National Park with its two saltwater lakes surrounded by dense pine forests, warrants an overnight stay.

Back on the mainland coast, the cheerful seaside resort of Cavtat and Trsteno Arboretum can also both be visited as day trips from Dubrovnik. Further north, Pelješac Peninsula is home to Ston, renowned for its excellent fresh shellfish, while Orebić is the main town in the Pelješac vineyards area. Across the narrow sea channel from Orebić, the island of Korčula is a must-see for its lovely capital, medieval Korčula Town, built on a tiny fortified peninsula.

Further out to sea, the underdeveloped island of Lastovo is a world unto itself. Despite officially belonging to South Dalmatia, both Korčula and Lastovo are served by ferry and catamaran from Split in Central Dalmatia, rather than Dubrovnik.

### Central Dalmatia
In Central Dalmatia, the monumental Roman city of Split is one of Croatia's most fascinating destinations. While the pedestrian-only old town lies within the ancient walls of Diocletian's Palace, looking directly out to sea, the modern high-rise suburbs extend along the coast and into the mountainous hinterland. With incoming ferries from Ancona

## Don't miss…

Numbers relate to the map on page 4.

in Italy, and regular daily ferries and catamarans to the nearby islands of Brač, Hvar and Vis, Split is a key transit point.

On Brač, the top resort is Bol, home to the stunning Zaltni Rat beach. On Hvar, you'll find Croatia's trendiest and most lovely island destination, the Venetian-era Hvar Town. Further out to sea, distant Vis produces organic wines and is much loved by sailing types for its authentic seafood eateries.

Back on the mainland coast, possible day trips south of Split include the seaside towns of Omiš and Makarska. Omiš lies at the mouth of the River Cetina, where you'll find organized whitewater rafting, while the cheerful resort of Makarska is at the foot of Mount Biokovo, whose rocky slopes offer a fierce challenge to seasoned hikers. North of Split, tiny medieval Trogir is home to an impressive cathedral. Further north still, industrial Šibenik is home to yet another noteworthy cathedral, and also makes a good base for visiting the waterfalls of Krka National Park.

### North Dalmatia

North Dalmatia's chief city, Zadar, centres on a charming old town built on a small fortified peninsula, packed with medieval buildings and several noteworthy Romanesque churches.

From Zadar, regular excursion boats take visitors on day trips around the dozens of rocky, arid, uninhabited islets that make up Kornati National Park. Those in search of a back-to-nature experience might rent a 'Robinson Crusoe-style' cottage here (see page 95), with no electricity or running water, but plenty of solitude. North Dalmatia's biggest and most visited island is Pag, a bizarre moonscape of rocky fields supporting the sheep that produce its highly regarded *paški sir*, a salty cheese similar to Italian pecorino. Also on Pag, which is joined to the mainland by a bridge, you'll find the commercial resort of Novalja, known for its 24-hour summer beach clubs.

North of Zadar, part of the Velebit mountain range falls within Paklenica National Park, a haven for hikers and free climbers. Here, the River Zrmanja is also a popular location for whitewater rafting.

## Getting to Dubrovnik and the Dalmatian Coast

### Air

**From UK and Ireland** **British Airways** flies to Dubrovnik from London Gatwick and to Zagreb from London Heathrow; **Croatian Airlines** flies to Zagreb from London Heathrow (with possible connecting flights to Dubrovnik, Pula, Split and Zadar); **EasyJet** flies to Dubrovnik from London Gatwick and Edinburgh and to Split from Bristol, London Gatwick or London Stansted; **Jet2.com** flies to Dubrovnik from Belfast, East Midlands, Edinburgh, Leeds Bradford, Manchester and Newcastle; to Pula from Glasgow, Leeds Bradford, Manchester and Newcastle; and to Split from Manchester; **Monarch** flies to Dubrovnik from Bristol, London Gatwick, Manchester; **Ryanair** flies to Zadar from Liverpool; **Thomsonfly** flies to Dubrovnik from London Gatwick and Manchester, and to Pula from Birmingham, London Gatwick and Manchester; and **Aer Lingus** flies to Dubrovnik from Dublin.

**From rest of Europe** There are direct flights to Croatia from most European capitals. Carriers include **Aeroflot**, **Air France/KLM**, **Austrian Airlines**, **Germanwings**, **Lufthansa**, **TAP Portugal** and **Turkish Airlines**.

**From North America** There are no direct flights from the US to Croatia.

---

### Airport information

**Zagreb Airport** (T01-456 2222, www.zagreb-airport.hr) has 2 banks, a post office, a duty-free shop, newsagents, a bar and restaurant, plus a number of rent-a-car companies, including **Hertz** (T01-456 2635, www.hertz.hr) and **HM Rentacar** (T01-370 4535, www.hm-rentacar.hr). Zagreb airport is 15 km south of the city centre. An airport bus, run by **Pleso** (T01-633 1999, www.plesoprijevoz.hr) makes regular runs between the airport and Zagreb Bus Station, a ticket costs 30Kn.

**Split Airport** (T021-203555, www.split-airport.hr) has a bank, a post office, a duty-free shop, newsagents, and bar and restaurant, plus car-hire companies including **Hertz** (T021-895230, www.hertz.hr) and **Uni Rent** (T021-895223, www.uni-rent.net). Split airport is 25 km west of the city centre. An airport bus, run by **Pleso** (T021-203119, www.plesoprijevoz.hr) runs at regular intervals between the airport and Split's bus station (in the city centre, opposite the ferry port), a ticket costs 30Kn.

**Dubrovnik Airport** (T020-773100, www.airport-dubrovnik.hr) has a bank, a duty-free shop, a bar, plus car-hire companies including **Avis** (T020-773811, www.avis.com.hr) and **Hertz** (T020-771568, www.hertz.hr). Dubrovnik airport is 21 km southeast of the city centre. An airport bus, run by **Atlas** (T020-442222, www.atlas-croatia.com) makes regular runs between the airport and Dubrovnik Bus Station, passing the outer walls of the old town en route, a ticket costs 35Kn.

**Zadar Airport** (T023-205800, www.zadar-airport.hr ) has a bank, a duty-free shop, a bar, plus car-hire companies including **Hertz** (T023-348400, www.hertz.hr). Zadar airport is 8 km east of the city centre. An airport bus, run by **Liburnija** (T023-343700, www.liburnija-zadar.hr) makes regular runs between the airport and Zadar's old bus station (on Liburnska obala, close to the old town) 25Kn.

## Rail

Regular daily international trains run direct to Zagreb from Venice, Ljubljana, Vienna, Budapest, Munich, Belgrade and Sarajevo.

The cheapest and fastest route from the UK is London–Paris–Venice–Zagreb, taking **Eurostar** ⓘ *www.eurostar.com*, through the Channel Tunnel. The entire journey takes about 39 hours and requires an overnight train. Prices vary greatly depending on how far in advance you book. For further details or information about alternative routes, contact **Rail Europe** ⓘ *www.raileurope.co.uk*, or check out the **Man in Seat Sixty-One** ⓘ *www. seat61.com*, an excellent website dedicated to travelling without flying.

If you are an EU passport holder and plan to travel across Europe to Croatia, consider buying a 'Global' **Inter Rail** ⓘ *www.interrailnet.com*, pass, offering unlimited second-class train travel in 30 countries. If you are 25 or under, a 15-day Global Inter Rail pass costs €307; if you are 26-59, it costs €435; and if you are 60 or over it costs €392.

## Road

There are good road links to Croatia from the neighbouring countries of Slovenia, Hungary, Bosnia and Herzegovina, and Serbia and Montenegro. Visitors arriving from Italy or Austria will pass through Slovenia.

**Eurolines** ⓘ *www.eurolines.co.uk*, runs a network of long-distance buses all over Europe. Though there is no longer a direct bus from the UK to Croatia, the journey is possible with changes in France or Germany.

## Sea

Croatia is well connected to Italy by overnight ferries the year through, and by additional fast daytime catamarans in summer.

**Jadrolinija** ⓘ *www.jadrolinija.hr*, runs regular year-round overnight services Ancona–Split, Ancona–Zadar and Dubrovnik–Bari. **Blue Line** ⓘ *www.blueline-ferries.com*, also cover the Ancona-Split route.

Regarding prices, if you travel Ancona–Split with Jadrolinija in peak season (August), expect to pay €48 for a one-way deck ticket (or €55 if you travel at the weekend), or €108.50 for a one-way ticket with a bed in a double cabin with a shower and WC (€124.50 at the weekend). A one-way ticket for a car is an extra €63.50 (or €73 at weekends).

In addition, **SNAV** ⓘ *snav.it*, operates fast, summer-only (mid-June to mid-September), daytime catamarans, with daily services for Ancona–Split. Expect to pay €69 Ancona–Split one-way (€138 return) for a foot passenger, plus €65 (return) for a car.

## Transport in Dubrovnik and the Dalmatian Coast

### Rail

All major Croatian cities, except Dubrovnik, are connected by rail. Train travel into more remote regions has been limited by topography, the rocky Dinaric Alps making it extremely difficult to build railways. Trains are operated by **Hrvatske Zeljeznice** ① *Croatian Railways, hznet.hr.* The most useful long-distance route is Zagreb–Split (5½ hours by day, eight hours by night) three trains daily, one is an overnight service with sleeping cars. For a one-way ticket expect to pay Zagreb–Split 180 Kn. A return ticket is sometimes, but not always, cheaper than two one-way tickets. The **InterRail Global pass** ① *interrailnet.com*, provides train travel throughout Croatia and the other 29 participating European countries. For national information contact **Zagreb Train Station** ① *T060-313333, www.hznet.hr.* **Split Train Station** ① *Obala Kneza Domagoja 9, T021-338470.*

### Road

**Bicycle** Croatia is a great destination for mountain biking but be aware that locals drive fast and occasionally a little recklessly on major mainland roads and are not used to cyclists. The islands, however, are perfect for exploring by bicycle.

**Bus/coach** Buses tend to be slightly faster and marginally more expensive than trains, and they are generally less comfortable. However, while train services are limited, by using the bus you can get from any major city to the most remote village, albeit with a few changes en route. There are numerous private companies, each operating on their own terms, so there's no such thing as an unlimited travel pass. Prices and quality of buses vary greatly from company to company, and a return ticket is sometimes, but not always, cheaper than two one-way tickets.

For national information contact **Zagreb Bus Station** ① *T060-313333, www.akz.hr.* **Split bus station** ① *Obala Kneza Domagoja 12, T060-327777, www.ak-split.hr.* **Dubrovnik bus station** ① *Obala pape Ivana Pavla II 44, T060-305070, www.libertasdubrovnik.com.* **Šibenik bus station** ① *Draga 14, T060-368368, www.atpsi.hr.* **Zadar bus station** ① *Ante Starčevića 1, T060-305305, www.liburnija-zadar.hr.*

**Car** Having a car obviously makes you more independent, so you can plan your itinerary more freely. However, it also creates various problems that you would not encounter if using public transport. Medieval walled cities such as Split and Dubrovnik are traffic free so you'll have to park outside the walls – even then, finding a place can be difficult (and expensive) as the more central parking spots are reserved for residents with permits. Having a car can also make ferry transfers to the islands extremely problematic: during high season be prepared to sit in queues for hours on end to get a place on the boat (there is no reservation system for vehicles: you buy a ticket and then it's first come, first aboard).

In summer 2005 two new motorways opened, connecting Zagreb and Rijeka, and Zagreb and Split. These are modern and fast, and you have to pay a toll to use them. The coastal road from Rijeka to Dubrovnik offers truly stunning views over the sea, but is twisty and tiring, and gets notoriously slippery after rain. On the islands, roads tend to be narrow and windy and are often less well maintained.

Petrol stations are generally open daily 0700-1800, and often until 2200 in summer. The larger cities and major international roads have 24-hour petrol stations.

**Hrvatski Autoklub (Croatian Automobile Club)** ⓘ *T1987, www.hak.hr,* offers a 24-hour breakdown service.

**Car hire**: Car hire is available at all the main airports. For one week in summer, expect to pay in the region of €380 for a small car such as a Fiat Seicento, or €505 for a Peugeot 208. Payments can be made by credit card, and your credit card number will be taken in lieu of a deposit. Most companies require drivers to be 21 or over.

## Sea

The Croatian Adriatic has 48 inhabited islands, many of which can be reached by ferry. There are regular connections between the mainland ports of Rijeka, Zadar, Split and Dubrovnik to nearby islands.

Prices are reasonable as the state-owned ferry company **Jadrolinija** ⓘ *www.jadrolinija.hr,* has been subsidized by the government in an attempt to slow down depopulation of islands. As well as connecting the islands, Jadrolinija operates a twice-weekly overnight coastal service (with cabins available) running from Rijeka to Dubrovnik, stopping at Split, Stari Grad (island of Hvar) and Korčula Town en route.

Sample high season prices are:

Rijeka–Split by ferry, one way, passenger 164Kn, car 448Kn; Split–Vis by ferry, one way, passenger 45Kn, car 308Kn; Split–Vis by high-speed catamaran one way, passenger 50Kn (no cars).

In addition to Jadrolinija, a number of smaller local companies run ferries and catamarans on certain routes In South Dalmatia, **Mediteranska Plovidba** ⓘ *www.medplov.hr,* runs a ferry from Orebić (mainland) to Korčula Town (Korčula) and **G&V Line** ⓘ *www.gv-line.hr,* connect Dubrovnik (mainland) to Sobra (Mljet) by fast catamaran, stopping at the Elafiti islands en route.

## Where to stay in Dubrovnik and the Dalmatian Coast

Along the coast, private accommodation, either in a rented room or apartment, is the best choice in terms of cost, facilities and insight into the way the locals live. However, if you feel like splashing out and being pampered here and there, the hotels listed in this guide have been selected for their authentic atmosphere and central location. There aren't any websites listing private accommodation, but local tourist offices often have details and their websites are listed throughout the book.

### Hotels

Croatian tourism dates back to the late-19th century when the region was under Austro-Hungary, and so along the coast you'll find a number of Vienna Secession-style hotels built for the Central European aristocracy of the time, such as several in Hvar Town, Korčula Town and Makarska.

During the tourist boom of the 1970s and 1980s, many of the older hotels were neglected in favour of large modern complexes, which sprang up in popular resorts such as Makarska, Bol, Hvar Town, Korčula Town and Dubrovnik. Although they tend to be vast and somewhat impersonal, these socialist-era hotels are equipped with excellent sports facilities, generally overlook the sea and are discreetly hidden by careful landscaping, a short walk from the centre of town. Over the last few years, some (most notably in Dubrovnik and Hvar Town) have been totally refurbished and have introduced chic minimalist design and wellness centres, bringing them into the luxury market.

The third and most recent breed of hotel are the small, private, family-run establishments, often in refurbished town houses, which have opened over the last decade and are now united under the **National Association of Small and Family Hotels**. For a full list, check out the website, omh.hr.

All hotels are officially graded by the Ministry of Tourism into five categories: five-star, luxury; four-star, de luxe; three-star, first class; two-star, moderate; and one-star, budget. Classified hotels are listed by the **Croatian National Tourist Board** ① *www.croatia.hr*, under their respective regions.

When referring to price lists, you will find that some hotels list half board and full board only. Simple 'bed and breakfast' works out only very slightly cheaper than half board, but is recommended as, by and large, hotel restaurants lack atmosphere, and the standard of the food unfortunately reflects the savings made in order to be able to offer cheap package deals. You are far better off eating out in local restaurants.

Last but not least, if you are staying on the coast it is well worth asking for a room with a sea view (most of which have balconies); it may cost a little more, but makes all the difference when you wake up in the morning.

### Private accommodation

Along the coast you will find a plethora of families offering *sobe* (rooms) and *apartmani* (apartments) for rent, usually with en suite bathrooms and simple self-catering facilities provided. These can be in anything from quaint, old stone cottages with gardens to modern concrete-block three-storey houses with spacious balconies. Hosts are generally welcoming and hospitable, and many visitors find a place they like and then return each summer.

Local tourist offices and travel agents have lists of recognized establishments and can arrange bookings for you. In busy areas, you'll also find people waiting for travellers at the

## Price codes

**Where to stay**

€€€€ over €300      €€€ €200-300

€€ €100-200      € under €100

Price codes refer to the cost of two people sharing a double room in high season.

**Restaurants**

€€€ over €40      €€ €20-40      € under €20

Price codes refer to the cost of a two-course meal with a drink, including service and cover charge.

ferry ports and bus stations, and offering rooms by word of mouth, but in this case you're not guaranteed to find the best standards.

Prices vary enormously depending on location, season and facilities provided, but you can expect to pay anything from 150-250Kn per person per day for a double room with an en suite bathroom, and anything from 400-1200Kn per day for a four-person apartment with a kitchen and dining area. Note that there is normally a 30% surcharge for stays of less than three nights.

A British-based operator specializing in quality private villas and apartments for holiday rentals in top Croatian resorts is **Croatian Villas Ltd** ① *Wood Green Business Centre, 5 Clarendon Rd, Wood Green, London N22 6XJ, T020-8888 6655, www.croatianvillas.com.*

### Robinson accommodation

So-called 'Robinson Crusoe' style accommodation started out on the Kornati islands, though it is gradually spreading to other isolated locations. As the term implies, this type of accommodation consists of a simple stone cottage, basically furnished and offering minimum modern comforts: gas lighting and water from a well. The beauty of these cottages lies in their detachment from the rest of the world – they are normally found on small unpopulated islands with no regular ferry links to the mainland, no shops and no cars. They are generally for rent on a weekly basis, and transport to them is arranged by the agencies responsible for letting them. For Croatian agencies specializing in these cottages, see page 98.

The British-based operator **Croatia for Travellers** ① *63 Therberton St, London N1 0QY, T020-7226 4460, www.croatiafortravellers.co.uk,* can also book a cottage for you – see the Kornati Islands section on their website.

### Agrotourism

An increasingly popular accommodation option is so-called agrotourism: farmhouses offering overnight accommodation and home cooking. This is a great solution for families with young children, as exploring the farm and getting to know the animals is guaranteed to go down well with kids. To date, the idea has only really taken off in Istria, but the potential is enormous.

Most of these establishments are off the beaten track (you normally need a car to reach them) and offer bed and breakfast deals in simply furnished rooms with en suite bathrooms. Many also have a restaurant area, often done out in rustic style, serving authentic local dishes (generally far superior to the food served in commercial restaurants), along with their own wine, cheese and olive oil. Some of the larger centres also offer a range of sporting activities such as horse riding and mountain biking.

# Lighthouses

Another novel and highly popular form of accommodation is the lighthouse. Along the Croatian coast, there are now 11 carefully restored lighthouses with apartments to rent on a weekly basis. Nine of these are on islands (you will be taken there and brought back by boat), and three on peninsulas along the mainland coast. In Istria, these include Savudrija (Umag), Rt Zub (Novigrad), Sv Ivan (Rovinj) and Porer (Pula).

Most lighthouses have one or two apartments sleeping anything from two to eight people, and several are still home to a resident lighthouse keeper. However, you can be sure of extreme isolation and minimum contact with the outside world, as most of them are located on lonely islets far out to sea. Each apartment has electricity, running water, TV and a fully equipped kitchen.

Bed linen and blankets are provided, but be sure to take a week's provisions as there will be no chance of shopping once you are there, unless you come to a special arrangement with local fishermen or the lighthouse keeper.

Prices vary greatly depending on the size of the apartment, location and season, but as an indicator the cost of renting a four-person apartment in the lighthouse of Sv Ivan, near Rovinj, are as follows: July to August €129 per day; June and September €99 per day; and during the rest of the year €79 per day. However, as this has become a hugely popular alternative, be sure to book several months in advance.

For further details contact **Adriatica Net** ① *Heinzelova 62a, Zagreb, T01-241 5611, www.adriatica.net*, who have an online booking service.

Prices vary greatly depending on the type of room, the location and season, but expect to pay anything from 180-320Kn per person per day for a double room (with an en suite bathroom) with breakfast in August.

For more information about farms and rural homes offering overnight accommodation and meals, enquire at the appropriate regional tourist boards.

## Camping

The sunny, dry climate and unspoilt nature make Croatia an ideal place for camping. Of at least 130 registered campsites, about 90% are on the mainland coast or on the islands, many backed by pinewoods overlooking the sea. Most operate from early May to early October, are well run and offer basic facilities such as showers and toilets and a small bar, while the larger ones may include restaurants and extensive sports facilities, such as scuba-diving courses and mountain bike rentals. Dalmatia might be less developed than Istria and Kvarner in terms of capacity and facilities provided, but is in many ways more attractive thanks to its rugged, untamed natural beauty. As in other European countries, camping outside of designated areas is prohibited.

For further information contact **Kamping Udruženje Hrvatske** ① *Croatian Camping Union, Pionirska 1, Poreč, T052-451324, www.camping.hr*. Their excellent website lists all official campsites, complete with contact details, facilities and prices. Naturist campsites are also listed and marked 'FKK'.

## Naturist camps

Naked bathing was first pioneered in Croatia in the early 20th century and Europe's first naturist campground opened here in 1953. Today there are 20 naturist campsites, almost all along the coast and on the islands, attracting visitors from Germany, Austria, the Netherlands, Italy and Slovenia, as well as other countries around the world.

For more information about naturism in Croatia, including a list of naturist camps with comments from people who have stayed at them, check out the **Croatia Naturally** website, cronatur.com.

## Youth hostels

There are now over 100 hostels dotted around the country, but only eleven are recognized by **Hostelling International (HI)** ① *www.hihostels.com*). Of these, only five are in Dalmatia, and they are in Zadar and Dubrovnik, plus a couple on the Makarska Rivijera (in Gradac and Zaostrog), and one in Stari Grad on the island of Hvar.

The remaining hostels (not recognized by HI) range from friendly low-key establishments to noisy and chaotic party dens. Nonetheless, all provide basic but comfortable dormitory-style accommodation (expect to pay around 120-180Kn per person per night, depending on the time of year), and some offer the option of half or full board. For information about HI-recoginsed hostels contact **Hrvatski Ferijalni i Hostelski Savez (Croatian Youth Hostel Association)** ① *Savska 5/1, 10000 Zagreb, T01-482 9294, www.hfhs.hr*.

# Food and drink in Dubrovnik and the Dalmatian Coast

## Food

Croatian cuisine can be divided into two main groups: Mediterranean along the coast and Continental in the inland regions. That said, each region has its own particular specialities reflecting its geography, history and culture. Croatia's highly complex past is clearly evident in its cooking, which displays the traces left by centuries of occupation by three foreign empires: the Venetians brought pasta and risotto to the coast; Austro-Hungary introduced paprika-flavoured goulash and strudel inland; and the Ottoman Turks bequeathed the region with sarma (stuffed sauerkraut rolls) and baklava.

Along the Dalmatian coast, simple, honest fish and seafood dishes top the menu. All ingredients are fresh and seasonal, so there's little attention paid to fussy preparation. The classic favourite is fresh fish, barbecued and served with olive oil and lemon, plus *blitva sa krumpirom* (swiss chard and potatoes with garlic and olive oil) as a side dish. Likewise, shellfish such as *kučice* (clams) and *škampi* (shrimps) are flashed over a hot flame with garlic, white wine and parsley, a method known as *na buzaru*, which cooks the seafood to a turn and produces a delicious rich sauce to mop up with bread. Worth mentioning here is that some of the best shellfish, notably *ostrige* (oysters) and *dagnje* (mussels), can be found in Ston on Pelješac Peninsula in South Dalmatia.

In summer, a popular and refreshing starter is *salata of hobotnice* (octopus salad) made from octopus, boiled potatoes, onion and parsley, dressed with olive oil and vinegar. Venetian influence is apparent in the abundance of risottos, the most popular being *crni rižot* (black risotto) made from cuttlefish ink, as well as *rižot frutti di mare* (seafood risotto), normally combining mussels, clams and prawns, and *rižot sa škampima* (shrimp risotto) invariably served with a splash of cream at the end. Pasta dishes are also served with a variety of seafood sauces, though the pasta is often overcooked by Italian standards. Another classic Dalmatian dish is *brodet*, a hearty mixed fish stew made with onions and tomatoes, and normally served with polenta. On the island of Hvar a local version of *brodet* is *gregada*, made with onions, potatoes and fresh herbs but no tomato.

When it comes to meat dishes, locals rave about *dalmatinski pršut*, smoked dried ham on a par with Italian prosciutto. It's normally served as an appetizer on a platter together with *paški sir* (sheep's cheese from the island of Pag) and a few olives. Meats such as steak, sausages and home-made burgers are invariably prepared on a charcoal fire and served with chips and a side salad (lettuce, cucumber and tomato). Another classic Dalmatian dish, brought to the area by the Venetians, is *pasticada*, beef stewed in sweet wine and served with *njoki* (gnocchi).

Lamb has a cult following throughout the Balkans, and in Croatia you'll see many roadside restaurants serving *janjetina* – whole lamb roast on a spit – especially in inland Dalmatia.

A special mention also needs to be given to the *peka*, a metal dome dating back to Illyrian times. Food is placed in a terracotta pot and covered entirely with a *peka*, which in turn is buried below white embers. Delicious casseroles of either octopus, veal or lamb can be prepared using this long, slow cooking method, though most restaurants that offer it stipulate that you should order a day in advance.

Desserts are limited, the standard offering being *palacinke* (pancakes), served either *sa orasima* (with walnuts), *sa marmeladom* (with jam) or *sa cokoladom* (with chocolate). In Dubrovnik, look out for *rožata*, similar to crème caramel.

If you visit the island of Vis, *pogača* makes a perfect snack – similar to Italian focaccia (from which it takes its name), it consists of a light bread base filled with tomato, onion and anchovy; you can buy it in several local bakeries.

## Drink

**Coffee and tea**  Meeting friends for *kava* (coffee) is something of a morning ritual. Many bars open as early as 0600, and are busy all day. While most people prepare Turkish coffee at home, cafés and bars serve Italian-style espresso and cappuccino. If you ask for *čaj* (tea) you will be given *šipak* (rosehip) served with lemon; if you want English-style tea ask for *indijski čaj sa mlijekom* (Indian tea with milk). Most cafés have tables outside, even in winter, and there is no extra charge for sitting down.

**Wine**  Croatian wines are little known abroad as they are exported in relatively small quantities, though some of them, such as the highly esteemed Dingač, are excellent. By and large the north produces whites and the south reds, though there are some exceptions.

Among the whites, names to look out for are: Pošip and Grk (from the island of Korčula), Vugava (island of Vis), Žlahtina (island of Krk), Malvazija (Istria), Graševina and Traminac (Slavonia). Of the reds, be sure to try: Dingač (Pelješac Peninsula), Plavac (islands of Hvar and Vis), Babić (Primošten) and Teran (Istria). Dalmatia also produces a rich sweet wine known as Prošek, similar to sherry.

To buy top wines at better prices, go direct to the producer. You will find vineyards open to the public on Pelješac Peninsula and the island of Hvar. On the island of Vis, some producers have opened shops where you can sample wine and then buy bottles to take home.

Lower-grade wines are bottled in one-litre bottles with a metal cap, while better wines come in 0.75 litre bottles with a cork. Sometimes you will find the same label on both, but the 0.75-litre bottle will be more expensive and of much higher quality. Most bars serve wine by the glass, either by the *dec* (1 dl) or *dva deca* (2 dl). In Dalmatia, *bevanda* (half white wine, half water) is a refreshing summer drink.

**Beer**  Beer was introduced to Croatia under Austro-Hungary, when the Hapsburgs built the first breweries to supply their soldiers. Light-coloured lager, served well chilled, is the most common sort of beer, with popular brands being Karlovačko, Kaltenburg, Laško Zlatorog and Ožujsko. Tomislav is a stout (dark beer) brewed in Zagreb. When you buy beer by the bottle, you pay a small deposit, which you can get back upon return of the empties and display of the receipt. Imported draught Guinness is popular but tends to be about three times the price of local beer.

**Spirits**  *Rakija*, a distilled spirit usually made from a grape base, was introduced to the region by the Turks, and is normally drunk as an aperitif before eating, but can also be taken as a digestive at the end of a meal. The most popular types are: *loza* (made from grapes), *travarica* (flavoured with aromatic grasses), *šljivovica* (made from plums) and *pelinkovac* (flavoured with juniper berries and bitter herbs, similar to Italian amaro). In addition, there are various regional specialities, such as *rogoš* (flavoured with carob) on the island of Vis. Imported spirits such as whisky and gin are popular but expensive.

# Menu reader

**blitva sa krumpirom** Swiss chard and potatoes with garlic and olive oil, a side dish

**brodet** a hearty Dalmatian fish stew made with onions and tomatoes, and served with polenta

**crni rižot** black risotto, made from cuttlefish ink

**dagnje** mussels

**friganje lignje** fried squid

**Hvarska gregada** a type of brodet made on the island of Hvar, using fish, onions, potatoes and fresh herbs, but no tomato

**janjetina** roast lamb, normally roast whole on a spit

**kobasice** sausages

**kućice** clams

**mješanja salata** mixed salad, usually lettuce, cucumber and tomato

**na buzaru** cooked with garlic, white wine and parsley to produce a delicious rich sauce

**ostrige** oysters

**palačinke** pancakes

**paški sir** a hard, salty sheep's cheese from the island of Pag

**pašticada s njokima** beef stewed in sweet wine and served with gnocchi

**peka** an ancient method of slow-cooking food (generally lamb, veal or octopus) when a terracotta pot is placed over white embers and covered by a metal dome; note that most restaurants require you to order peka dishes at least one day in advance

**pršut** smoked dried ham similar to Italian prosciutto

**ražnjiči** kebabs

**riba na žaru** barbecued fish, normally drizzled with olive oil and served with a wedge of lemon

**rižot frutti di mare** seafood risotto, normally combining mussels, clams and prawns

**rižot sa škampima** shrimp risotto, invariably served with a splash of cream at the end

**salata od hobotnice** octopus salad, made from octopus, boiled potatoes, onion and parsley, dressed with olive oil and vinegar

**rožata** a Dubrovnik speciality, similar to crème caramel

**škampi** shrimps

**škampi na buzaru** shrimps cooked in garlic, white wine and parsley to produce a delicious rich sauce

**sladoled** ice cream

## Eating out

For a full blown lunch or dinner, visit a *restoran* (restaurant), where you can expect formal service and a menu including a wide range of Croatian dishes. Most restaurants are open 1200-1500 and 1900-2300, and many, especially along the coast, have a large terrace for open-air dining through the summer months. For a simpler meal, try a *gostionica*, a place you can also go just to drink. There may not be a written menu, but many *gostionice* in Dalmatia serve *merenda* (a hearty cut-price brunch), offer daily specials chalked up on a board, and sometimes have a set three-course meal, which works out very cheap. Service will be less formal, but you can often land some excellent home cooking, and they tend to stay open all day, Monday to Saturday 0800-2300. The term *konoba* (in Dalmatia) was originally associated with a place for making and storing wine, but it is now used by many rustic-style restaurants serving local specialities. Some open in the evenings only and may stay open for late-night drinking. Most towns have a pizzeria, and some serve excellent pizza, comparable to the best in Italy. A few also offer a choice of substantial salads and a limited selection of pasta dishes.

For something sweet, call at a *slasti arnica*. Many are run by Albanians (one of former Yugoslavia's ethnic minorities) and they offer eastern goodies such as baklava, along with a selection of *sladoled* (ice creams). Most are open 0800-2000, and serve coffee, tea and fruit juices, but no alcohol.

## Eating in

If you opt for private accommodation you will probably have self-catering facilities. All cooking utensils and kitchen equipment such as pans, bowls, plates, glasses, cups and cutlery will be provided: if anything is missing ask your host and they will give you anything extra you require. Occasionally basics such as sugar, salt and pepper are present – normally left by the people who were there before you.

You will probably also be supplied with a *džezver* – a metal coffee pot with a handle, used for preparing Turkish-style coffee, which is usually drunk here rather than instant, filter or espresso coffee. Vacuum-packed ground coffee can be bought in general stores.

# Festivals in Dubrovnik and the Dalmatian Coast

## January
**Nova Godina** (1st) Croats celebrate the arrival of New Year with open-air concerts and fireworks in all the big cities: in Split on the Riva (seafront promenade) and in Dubrovnik on Placa in the old town.

## February
**Sveti Vlaho** (3rd) In Dubrovnik, the life of Saint Blaise, the city's patron, is celebrated with a religious procession around the old town; the saint's remains, in the form of relics, take pride of place. During the time of the republic, those prisoners who did not present a threat to public safety were released on this day to participate in the festivities.

**Karneval** (around Shrove Tue) In the days leading up to Lent, many towns and villages in Croatia celebrate carnival. The biggest celebrations take place in Rijeka www.rijecki-karneval.hr) in the Kvarner region. In Dalmatia, carnival is celebrated in Dubrovnik with a masked ball on the final night. While in Lastovo Town, on the island of Lastovo, on Shrove Tue locals make a straw figurine, known as Poklad, who is tied to a rope and hoisted up and down the hill in the centre of town 3 times, with fireworks attached to his boots. He is put on a donkey and taken to the square in front of the parish church where he is burnt. In Split, carnival is known as maškare. On the evening of Shrove Tue, locals take part in a costume procession, culminating in the burning of Krnjo (an effigy symbolizing the past year's evils) on the seafront.

## March/April
**Sveti Križ** (night before Good Fri) On the island of Hvar, the Carrying of the Holy Cross is an all-night procession connecting the six villages of Jelsa, Pitve, Vrisnik, Svirče, Vrbanj and Vrboska. Activity begins in the late evening, when groups set out from each parish church, led by a much-honoured young man carrying a large wooden crucifix. The parties pass through each of the other villages in turn, to return to their respective churches for sunrise on Good Fri morning.

## April
**Croatia Boat Show** (www.croatiaboatshow. com). Held in Split, this 1-week boat show sees the city's seafront promenade extended over the water to create a floating stage, with piers and mooring spaces accommodating several hundred luxurious sailing boats and speedboats. In the past, the event has attracted thousands of visitors from countries all over the world however, in 2012 it was cancelled, and its future is now uncertain.

## May
**Sudamje** (7th) In Split, the bones of St Domnius, the city's patron saint, are on display in the cathedral, and a festival takes place on the Riva (seafront), with stands selling handmade wooden objects and basketry. It is a local public holiday.

## June/July
**Dubrovnik Opera Festival** (Jun, www. dubrovnik-opera-festival-com). A 4-day opera festival, staged in the courtyard of the Rector's Palace.

## July/August
**Garden Festivals** (Jul and Aug; www. thegardenfestival.eu) A series of open-air music festivals are staged by the sea in Tisno on the island of Murter (in the past they were in Petrčane, close to Zadar, but that venue is no longer functioning).
**Zrče Beach Festivals** (Jul-Aug). A series of multi-day music festivals take place on Zrče beach in Novalja on the island of Pag, with the programme changing each summer.
**Dubrovnik Summer Festival** (mid-Jul to mid-Aug; www.dubrovnik-festival.hr)

The international Dubrovnik Summer Festival hosts drama, ballet, concerts and opera at open-air venues in the old town.

**Ethnoambient Salona** (late-Jul; www. ethnoambient.net)  Held on the Salona archaeological site near Split, this 3-day open-air event attracts musicians from as far afield as Scotland, Portugal and Greece.

**Music Evenings of St Donat** (mid-Jul to mid-Aug; www.donat-festival.com)  In Zadar, the Musical Evenings see medieval, Renaissance and baroque music concerts staged inside the deconsecrated Church of St Donat.

**Festival Dalmatinskih Klapa** (Jul; www.fdk. hr). In Omiš, the 3-week Dalmatian Klapa Festival aims to preserve this form of harmony singing and promote new songs. It now attracts about 80 groups comprising more than a 1000 singers. Performances are held at open-air locations around town and inside the parish church.

**Splitsko Ljeto** (Jul and Aug; www.splitsko-ljeto.hr)  The Split Summer Festival hosts opera, theatre and dance at open-air venues within the walls of Diocletian's Roman Palace.

**Ston Summer Festival** (late Jul-late Aug, www.ston.hr). In Veli Ston on Pelješac, this summer festival stages open-air evening concerts and plays in the old town.

**Terraneo** (mid-Aug, www.terraneofestival. com). In Šibenik, a 4-day alternative music festival with an impressive international line-up and a large campsite.

**Faros Marathon** (last weekend of Aug) Held in Stari Grad on the island of Hvar, this swimming competition sees competitors from as far afield as France and Russia swim 16 km, from town to the end of the bay and back again.

**Film Forum Zadar** (late-Aug, www.film forumzadar.com). A 1-week international film festival held in Zadar.

## September

**Epidaurus Festival** (www.epidaurusfestival. com). In Cavtat, a 10-day international music and art festival.

## December

**Sveti Nikola** (6th)  St Nicholas, the patron saint of sailors, fishermen and travellers, is honoured with the ceremonial burning of a fishing boat in front of St Nicholas' Church in Komiža on the island of Vis.

# Essentials A-Z

### Accident and emergency
In the case of an emergency requiring police attention, dial 192. For an ambulance, dial 94.

### Electricity
Croatia functions on 220 volts AC, 50Hz; plugs have 2 round pins (as in most of continental Europe).

### Health
Most EU countries have a reciprocal healthcare agreement with Croatia, meaning that you pay a basic minimum for a consultation and hospital treatment is free if you can show your European Health Insurance Card (EHIC).

For minor complaints visit a *ljekarna* (pharmacy), recognized by its green cross outside; most are open Mon-Fri 0800-1900 and Sat 0800-1400, and in larger cities at least one will be open 24 hrs. In an emergency, go to *hitno pomoč* (casualty). Dial 94 for an ambulance.

### Language
Croatian belongs to the South Slavic branch of the Slavic group of languages – a similar language is spoken by Serbs, Montenegrins and Bosnians. Most people working in tourism, as well as the majority of younger Croatians, speak good English, so you won't have much of a problem communicating unless you get off the beaten track. If you do make the effort to learn a few words and phrases, though, your efforts are likely to be rewarded with a smile of appreciation.

### Money
The official currency is the kuna (Kn), which is divided into 100 lipa. It is now possible to buy kune outside Croatia, though you may have to order them from your bank several days in advance, as there is a relitevly low demand for the currency. Although Croatia

is scheduled to join the EU in July 2013, it will not adopt the Euro immediately.

In the meantime, the euro is the most readily accepted foreign currency. Most towns and villages, even on the islands, have a banka (bank), generally open Mon-Fri 0700-1900 and Sat 0700-1300, and most have an ATM too. Major credit cards (**American Express**, **Diners Club**, **MasterCard** and **Visa**) are widely accepted.

Croatia is not a cheap option, with hotel and restaurant prices similar to Greece. Prices rise significantly through Jul and Aug with an influx of Italian and German tourists. Private rooms are the best source of low-cost, clean, comfortable accommodation – expect to pay anything between 300Kn and 500Kn for a double, depending on the place, time of year and furnishing. At the really top-class luxury hotels in Dubrovnik and Hvar Town, you can expect to pay over 2000Kn for a double room in high season. Prices in Dubrovnik have escalated out of all proportion, so that even a cup of coffee now costs double what it would cost anywhere else in Croatia. Happily, public transport (buses, trains and ferries) throughout the country is still very cheap by EU standards.

### Opening times
Many museums are closed on Mon and public holidays.

### Safety
Despite the negative image created by the war, Croatia has a lower crime rate than most other European countries. Rare cases of violent crime are usually targeted at specific persons connected to organized crime. Foreigners do not appear to be singled out.

Although military action connected to the war ended in 1995, the problem of landmines, mostly along the former front lines in eastern Slavonia and the Krajina, remains. De-mining is not complete: if you are passing through such areas, exercise caution and do not stray from known safe roads and paths.

## Time
GMT+1.

## Tipping
Tips are not included on bills. At the end of a good meal at a restaurant it is customary to leave 10% extra if you are satisfied with the service. Bar staff do not expect tips.

## Tourist information
The Croatian National Tourist Board, croatia.hr, covers the whole country.

All the major cities and even most small towns along the coast and on the islands have a *turistički ured* (tourist office), see the relevant sections for the contact details of these offices. They provide information about local hotels, sports facilities and public transport, and most can help you find self-catering accommodation. The larger tourist offices provide maps and sightseeing information.

## Visas
EU citizens do not need a visa but do require a passport to enter Croatia for stays for up to 90 days. Once Croatia joins the EU in Jul 2013, the usual EU regulations will apply regarding longer stays. For further details, visit the Croatian Ministry of Foreign Affairs website, www.mvp.hr.

## Contents

## Footprint features

Dubrovnik & South Dalmatian Coast

## Dubrovnik → *For listings, see pages 45-54.*

Lying 216 km southeast of Split, backed by rugged limestone mountains and jutting out into the Adriatic Sea, Dubrovnik, for centuries the independent Republic of Ragusa, is one of the world's finest and best-preserved fortified cities. Its gargantuan walls and medieval fortress towers enclose the historic centre, which is filled with terracotta-roof town houses and monuments such as the 15th-century Rector's Palace, two monasteries with cloistered gardens and several fine baroque churches with copper domes. The old town is traversed by the main pedestrian promenade, Stradun (Placa), which is paved with glistening white limestone and lined with open-air cafés. In 1979, the city became a UNESCO World Heritage Site. A recent new attraction is the Dubrovnik Cable Car, which transports visitors to the peak of Mount Srđ, for amazing views down onto town and out to sea.

Tourism has a long history here and the museums, churches, hotels and restaurants are all well geared to foreign visitors – beware that in Dubrovnik you can expect to pay almost double what you would anywhere else in Croatia. Dubrovnik is considered one of Europe's most exclusive destinations, heaving with visitors through high season and attracting more than its share of international celebrities – Francis Ford Coppola and Tina Turner visited in summer 2012. Cruise ships en route from Venice to the Greek islands make it a port of call, several of the country's plushest and most expensive hotels can be found here, and it's the main base for charter companies hiring out yachts in South Dalmatia.

# 1 Dubrovnik orientation

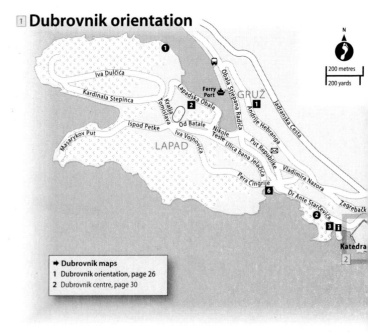

→ Dubrovnik maps
1  Dubrovnik orientation, page 26
2  Dubrovnik centre, page 30

## Arriving in Dubrovnik

**Getting there** Dubrovnik Airport ① *T020-773100, www.airport-dubrovnik.hr*, is 21 km southeast of the city centre and is served by regular shuttle bus (35Kn). The **bus station** is at ① *Obala pape Ivana Pavla II 44, T060-305070, www.libertasdubrovnik.com*.

Dubrovnik's port is at Gruž, 3 km west of the old town. **Jadrolinija** ① *www.jadrolinija.hr*, operates daily local ferries from Dubrovnik to the nearby Elafiti islands. Jadrolinija also runs a ferry to Sobra on Mljet, while **G&V Line** ① *gv-line.hr*, cover the same route by catamaran (Nona Ana), stopping at the Elafiti islands en route. Lastovo is not connected to Dubrovnik by boat, instead it is served by ferry and catamaran from Split (Central Dalmatia). Jadrolonija also runs a coastal ferry several times weekly from Dubrovnik to Rijeka (Kvarner), stopping at the islands of Korčula and Hvar, and at Split, en route. The same ferry sometimes (three times per week in May; six times per week in August) also does an overnight trip from Dubrovnik to Bari (Italy). Note that there is no train service to Dubrovnik.

**Tourist information** The new walk-in **tourist information centre** ① *Brsalje 5, T020-312011*, is close to Pile Gate just outside the city walls. In addition, there is a **tourist information centre** ① *Obala S Radića 32, T020-417983*, close to the ferry landing station in Gruž harbour. The following websites are also useful: **Dubrovnik City Tourist Board** ① *tzdubrovnik.hr*, and **Dubrovnik County Tourist Board** ① *www.visitdubrovnik.hr*.

For further information see Getting to Dubrovnik and the Dalmatian Coast, page 8, and Transport, page 53.

**Where to stay** 🛏
Bellevue **6**
Berkeley **1**
Lapad **2**
MirO Studio
  Apartments **3**

**Restaurants** 🍴
Orsan **1**
Tovjerna Sesame **2**

### Gradske Zidine

① *T020-324641, www.citywallsdubrovnik.hr, May-Sep daily 0800-1900, Oct-Apr daily 1000-1500, 70Kn.*

To reach the city walls, climb the steps immediately to your left after passing through Pile Gate. The highlight of any visit to Dubrovnik has to be a walk around the city walls. To walk the full circuit, 2 km, you should allow at least an hour.

The walls, as they stand today, follow a ground plan laid down in the 13th century. However, the fall of Constantinople to the Turks in 1453 sent panic waves throughout the Balkans, and Ragusa hastily appointed the renowned Renaissance architect, Michelozzo di Bartolomeo (1396-1472) from Florence, to further reinforce the city fortifications with towers and bastions. On average the walls are 24 m high and up to 3 m thick on the seaward side, 6 m on the inland side.

# Dubrovnik under siege

In the early 1990s, when the war of independence broke out, Yugoslav forces placed the city under siege. From November 1991 to May 1992, the ancient fortifications stood up to bombardments; fortunately none of the main monuments were seriously damaged, though many of the terracotta rooftops were blasted to fragments. The international media pounced on the story, and it was the plight of Dubrovnik that turned world opinion against Belgrade, even though less glamorous cities, such as Vukovar in Eastern Slavonia were suffering far worse devastation and bloodshed. During the second half of the 1990s, money poured in from all over world and today, thanks to careful restoration work (costing an estimated US$10 million), few traces of war damage remain and Dubrovnik is once again a fashionable, high-class holiday resort.

## Vrata od Pila

There are two gates into the city walls – Pile Gate is to the west. The name Pile comes from the Greek *pili* meaning 'gate'. During the time of the republic, they were closed each evening at 1800 and reopened at 0600 the next morning; the keys were kept under the custody of the rector. Pile Gate, as it stands today, combines a stone bridge, a wooden drawbridge on chains, and an outer Renaissance portal from 1537 followed by a Gothic inner gate from 1460. From May to October, guards in period costume stand vigilant by both gates, just as they would have done when the city was an independent republic.

## Velika Onofrio Fontana

ⓘ *Poljana Paska Miličevića.*

Located in the square just inside Pile Gate, Onofrio's Greater Fountain was part of the city's water supply system, designed by the Neapolitan builder Onofrio de la Cava to bring water from the River Dubrovačka 20 km away. It was completed in 1444. Topped with a dome, water runs from 16 spouting masks around the sides of the fountain. Originally it would have been decorated with ornate sculptures, which were unfortunately destroyed during the earthquake of 1667.

## Stradun

Up until the 12th century, Stradun (also known as Placa) was a shallow sea channel, separating the island of Laus from the mainland. After it was filled in, it continued to divide the city socially for several centuries, with the nobility living in the area south of Stradun, while the commoners lived on the hillside to the north. It forms the main thoroughfare through the old town, running 300 m from Pile Gate to Ploče Gate. The glistening white limestone paving dates from 1468, though the stone buildings to each side were constructed after the earthquake of 1667. While the upper levels were residential, the ground floors were used as shops. Still today Stradun serves as the city's main public gathering place, where locals conduct their morning and evening promenades and meet at rather pricey open-air cafés.

## Franjevačka Samostan

ⓘ *Placa 2, T020-321410, malabraca.wix.com, Apr-Oct daily 0900-1800, Nov-Mar daily 0900-1700, 30Kn.*

The Franciscan Monastery complex centres on a delightful cloister from 1360 – late Romanesque arcades are supported by double columns, each crowned with a set of grotesque figures, beside an internal garden filled with palms and Mediterranean shrubs. There's a small museum displaying early laboratory equipment, ceramic bowls and old medical books from the pharmacy, founded by the monks in 1318 and said to be the oldest institution of its kind in Europe.

## Palača Sponza

ⓘ *Luža, T020-321032, May-Oct 0900-2100, Nov-Apr 0900-1500, free (ground floor only).*

At the east end of Placa, the Sponza Palace was designed by Paskoje Miličević in 1522 and displays a blend of Renaissance arches on the lower level and Venetian-Gothic windows on the first floor. Through the centuries it has been used as a customs office and the city mint (Ragusa minted its own money, a convertible currency known as the *perpera*) though it now houses the state archives. The ground floor is open for temporary exhibitions, and during the Summer Festival concerts take place in the internal courtyard. This is one of the few buildings to survive the 1667 earthquake.

## Dominikanski Samostan

ⓘ *Sv Dominika 4, T020-321423, May-Oct daily 0900-1800, Nov-Apr 0900-1700, 20Kn.*

Behind the Sponza Palace, in a passageway leading to Ploče Gate, the Dominican Monastery centres on a 15th-century late-Gothic cloister, designed by the Florentine architect Michelozzo di Bartolomeo (1396-1472) and planted with orange trees. The east wing of the complex houses a museum exhibiting 15th- and 16th-century religious paintings by members of the Dubrovnik School – notably a triptych featuring the *Virgin and Child* by Nikola Božidarević and a polyptych centring on the *Baptism of Christ* by Lovro Dobričević – as well as works by the city's goldsmiths and reliquaries collected by the monks through the centuries. The rather plain interior of the monastery church is worthwhile for the *Miracle of St Dominic* by Vlaho Bukovac (1855-1922), a local painter from Cavtat.

## Vrata od Ploča

The main entrance into the old town from the east, Ploče Gate, like Pile Gate, combines a 15th-century stone bridge with a wooden drawbridge and a stone arch bearing a statue of St Blaise.

## Crkva Svetog Vlaha

ⓘ *Luža, daily 0800-1200 and 1630-1900.*

Opposite the Sponza Palace, the baroque Church of St Blaise, built between 1705 and 1717, replaced an earlier 14th-century structure destroyed by fire following the earthquake of 1667. It is dedicated to the city's patron saint, St Blaise, and on the high altar stands a silver statue of him, holding a model of the city from the 16th century, which is paraded around town each year on 3 February, the Day of St Blaise. The stained-glass windows, a feature rarely seen in churches in southern Europe, were added in the 1970s.

### Knežev Dvor

ⓘ *Pred Dvorom 3, T020-321497, May-Sep daily 0900-1800, Oct-Apr Mon-Sat 0900-1600, 35Kn.*
Behind the Church of St Blaise, the Rector's Palace is the building where the citizen holding the one-month term as rector was obliged to reside during his time in office; he could only leave for official business and his family remained in their own home.

The building dates from the 15th-century, though the arcaded loggia and internal courtyard, combining late-Gothic and early-Renaissance styles, were largely built after the 1667 earthquake.

In the courtyard (where classical music concerts are held during the Summer Festival) stands a bust of Miho Pracat (1528-1607), a powerful merchant and ship owner from the nearby island of Lopud, who left his wealth to the republic for charitable purposes when he died. When the bust was erected in 1638, he became the only man to be honoured in such a way – the production of statues of local personalities was generally forbidden to prevent the cult of hero worship. Next to the courtyard are a series of large rooms where the Great Council and Senate held their meetings; over the entrance to the meeting halls a plaque reads *Obliti privatorum publica curate* (Forget private affairs, and get on with public matters).

Upstairs, the rector's living quarters now accommodate the *Gradski Muzej* (City Museum), offering an idea of how people once lived in the Republic of Ragusa. Exhibits include paintings by Venetian and Dalmatian artists, period furniture, costumes and a

## ② Dubrovnik centre

➡ **Dubrovnik maps**
1  Dubrovnik orientation, page 26
2  Dubrovnik centre, page 30

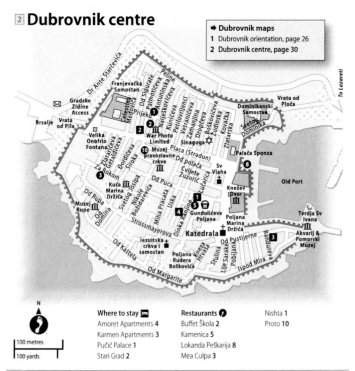

**Where to stay** 🛏
Amoret Apartments **4**
Karmen Apartments **3**
Pučić Palace **1**
Stari Grad **2**

**Restaurants** 🍴
Buffet Škola **2**
Kamenica **5**
Lokanda Peškarija **8**
Mea Culpa **3**

Nishta **1**
Proto **10**

curious collection of clocks, each one stopped at 1745, the hour Napoleon's men took the city on 31 January 1806, symbolizing the fall of the republic.

## Gundulićeva Poljana

Each morning, from Monday to Saturday, an open-air fruit and vegetable market sets up on Gundulićeva Poljana, west of the Rector's Palace. Come sunset, the market stalls are packed away and several restaurants put out tables in their place. In the middle of the square is a bronze statue of the Ragusan writer Ivan Gundulić (1589-1638), completed by Ivan Rendić in 1892. Gundulić is best known for his epic poem *Osman* (1626), describing the Poles' victory over the Turks, and the four sides of the stone pedestal upon which the statue is mounted are decorated with reliefs of scenes from the poem.

## Katedrala

ⓘ *Poljana Marina Držića, T020-323459 (Treasury), May-Sep Mon-Sat 0900-1700, Sun 1000-1700; Oct-Apr Mon-Sat 1000-1200 and 1500-1700, Sun 1100-1200 and 1500-1700, 15Kn (Treasury).*

The original 12th-century cathedral, said to have been sponsored in part by Richard the Lionheart of England out of gratitude for having been saved from a shipwreck on the nearby island of Lokrum on his return from the Crusades in 1192, was destroyed in the 1667 earthquake. What you see today is a splendid baroque structure with three aisles and a cupola, designed by Andrea Buffalini of Rome in 1671. The light but rather bare interior contains a number of paintings, notably a large polyptych above the main altar depicting *The Assumption of Our Lady*, attributed to the Venetian master, Titian (1485-1576). Adjoining the cathedral, the rich Treasury displays 138 gold and silver reliquaries, originating primarily from the East and brought to the city by the local seafarers. Pride of place is held by the skull of St Blaise in the form of a bejewelled Byzantine crown; an arm and a leg of the saint are also on show, likewise encased in elaborately decorated golden plating.

## Akvarij

ⓘ *Damjana Jude 2, Tvrdja Sv Ivana (St John's Fortress), T020-323125, May-Sep daily 0900-2100, Oct-Apr Tue-Sun 1000-1300, 30Kn.*

The St John's Fortress complex, behind the cathedral, guards the entrance to the old city port. At night, the port used to be closed by stretching a chain from the fortress to Kaše, a breakwater built in the 15th century. The ground floor of the fortress now houses the Aquarium, where several saltwater pools and 27 well-lit tanks display an impressive variety of Adriatic fish including ray and small sharks, and other underwater life such as octopuses, sponges and urchins.

## Pomorski Muzej

ⓘ *Tvrdja Sv Ivana (St John's Fortress), Damjana Jude 2, T020-323904, May-Sep Tue-Sun 0900-1800, Oct-Apr Tue-Sun 0900-1600, 40Kn.*

Above the Aquarium, on the first floor of St John's Fortress, the Maritime Museum traces Dubrovnik's development into one of the world's most important seafaring nations, with exhibits including intricately detailed model ships, as well as engine room equipment, sailors' uniforms, paintings and maps. There are also sections dedicated to the age of steam, the Second World War, and sailing and navigation techniques.

## Jezuitska Crkva i Samostan

ⓘ *Poljana R Boškovića, daily 0900-1200 and 1500-1900.*

Completed in 1725, the Jesuit Church is Dubrovnik's largest and was modelled on the baroque Il Gesu in Rome, which was designed by Giacomo da Vignola in the mid-16th century. To reach it, follow Uz Jezuite and climb an imposing staircase dating from 1738, often compared to Rome's Spanish Steps. Next to the church stands the Jesuit College, where many illustrious local citizens were educated.

## Muzej Pravoslavne Crkve

ⓘ *Od Puča 8, T020-323283, summer Mon-Sat 0900-1400, winter Mon-Fri 0900-1400, 10Kn.*

Next door to the Orthodox Church, built in 1877, stands the Orthodox Church Museum, with a collection of 77 religious icons, originating largely from the island of Crete and the Bay of Kotor (a short distance down the coast in Montenegro) and painted between the 15th and 19th centuries.

## War Photo Limited

ⓘ *Antuninska 6, between Placa and Prijeko, T020-322166, www.warphotoltd.com, Jun-Sep daily 0900-2100; May and Oct Tue-Sun 1000-1600; Nov-Apr closed, 30Kn.*

This is a beautifully designed two-floor gallery dedicated to photo-journalism from war zones around the world. It has staged exhibitions from Afghanistan, Iraq, former Yugoslavia, Israel and Palestine and is emotionally gruelling but well worth visiting.

## Dubrovnik Cable Car

ⓘ *Frana Supila 35a, T020-325393, www.dubrovnikcablecar.com, Jun-Aug 0900-2400, Sep 0900-2200, Oct and Apr-May 0900-2000, Nov and Feb-Mar 0900-1700, Dec-Jan 0900-1600, 50Kn (one-way).*

Opened in July 2010, this modern cable car departs from a lower station, just outside the old town, whizzing visitors to the peak of Mount Srdj (405 m) in just three minutes. From the top, where you'll find a café, restaurant and viewing platform, you have an amazing bird's eye perspective down onto the old town and out to sea.

## Islet of Lokrum

ⓘ *www.lokrum.com, during the summer, regular taxi boats (50Kn) shuttle visitors back and forth from the old port.*

East of the city walls, just a 15-minute boat ride from the old port, you'll find the lush island of Lokrum. A Benedictine Monastery was founded here in 1023, and legend has it that when French authorities began closing down religious institutions in the early 19th century, local Benedictines placed a curse upon anyone who should try to possess Lokrum. A succession of subsequent owners died mysterious and horrific deaths, one being the unfortunate Archduke Maximilian von Hapsburg, who bought the island in 1859, only to be taken prisoner and shot in Mexico in 1867. Before departing, Maximilian built a summer home here, set amid a Botanical Garden filled with exotic plants and peacocks, which can still be seen today – in fact the peacocks have multiplied profusely. Even now, locals remain superstitious about Lokrum, and while it is a popular bathing area during daylight hours, no one stays on the island after sunset.

There are some decent beaches on the southwest side of the island, plus a small saltwater lake, and beyond it an area reserved for nudists.

You'll find a restaurant within the former monastery, and there's also a seasonal café.

## Beaches

The main bathing area close to the old town is Eastwest Beach Club between the city walls and Lazareti, while a little further down the coast you'll find Sveti Jakov beach in a small bay backed by cliffs and approached down a long flight of steps. The best bathing spot on Lapad Peninsula is Lapad Cove, where there's a pebble beach in a deep bay.

## Around Dubrovnik → *For listings, see pages 45-54.*

### Trsteno Arboretum

ⓘ *24 km northwest of Dubrovnik, T020-751019, May-Oct daily 0700-1900, Nov-Apr daily 0800-1600, 35Kn, all buses heading north up the coast from Dubrovnik stop in Trsteno (45 mins), though you should tell the driver in advance otherwise he may drive straight on.*

The small village of Trsteno is on the main coastal road. Its 16th-century Renaissance arboretum, one of the oldest and most beautiful landscaped parks in Croatia, makes a pleasant outing at any time of the year, though the trees and planting are at their most attractive in spring and autumn.

The park, laid out in the grounds of a Renaissance villa belonging to the Gucetić family, was designed to emphasize the magnificence of its clifftop setting: a series of terraces tumble down to the sea, offering stunning views over Trsteno's harbour and out across the water to the Elafiti Islands.

Traditionally the men of Trsteno were sailors, and wherever they went in the world they would collect seeds and saplings for the Gucetić gardens. Today, the arboretum contains pines from Japan, palms from Mexico and cypress trees from various parts of the Mediterranean, as well as pomegranate, almond and lemon trees, and exotic climbing plants such as sweet jasmine and passion flower. Pride of place is taken by a 500-year-old plane tree, with a 12-m circumference and boughs so massive that one of them has to be supported by a concrete pillar.

Behind the villa stands an ornate water garden from 1736, featuring a grotto presided over by baroque statues of Neptune and two nymphs, and a pool fed with water from a trickling stream.

On October 1991, during the war of independence, the arboretum was shelled from the sea and part of the pinewoods was consumed by fire. However, careful restoration work has covered up the worst of the damage, and today Trsteno still evokes the sophisticated lifestyle of Renaissance Dubrovnik.

### Cavtat

The pretty fishing town of Cavtat, 17 km southeast of Dubrovnik, is Croatia's southernmost seaside resort. It was originally founded by ancient Greeks from Issa (Island of Vis, Central Dalmatia) and was called Epidauros. During the 15th century, it was incorporated into the Republic of Dubrovnik. Town walls were erected, and a rector installed to govern the rural hinterland region known as Konavle. Tourism began in the early 1900s under Austro-Hungary; during the 1980s several large hotel complexes were built and Cavtat turned into a popular package resort. For a year from October 1991, it was occupied by the JNA (Yugoslav Peoples' Army). The town suffered minimal material damage, though many houses in Konavle were looted and burnt during this period.

Today café life centres on the palm-lined seafront promenade giving onto a deep curving bay protected by a peninsula. Most of the hotels are located north of town, set amid lush Mediterranean vegetation and overlooking a second bay.

**Tourist information Cavtat tourist office** ① *Zidine 6, T020-479025, www.tzcavtat-konavle.hr.*

**Baltazar Bogišić Collection** ① *Obala Ante Starčevića 18, T020-478556, Mon-Sat 0900-1300, 15Kn.* Housed within the 16th-century Renaissance Rector's Palace, this collection includes drawings by Croatian and foreign artists, and an impressive canvas, *Carnival in Cavtat*, by Vlaho Bukovac. There is also a lapidarium with Roman stone pieces from the first century AD and a display of old coins, some from the Republic of Ragusa (Dubrovnik).

**Vlaho Bukovac Gallery** ① *Bukovčeva 5, T020-478646, www.kuca-bukovac.hr, May-Oct Tue-Sat 0900-1300, 1600-2000, Sun 1600-2000; Nov-Apr Tue-Sat 0900-1300, 1400-1700, Sun 1400-1700, 20Kn.* The birthplace of the realist painter Vlaho Bukovac (1855-1922) has been turned into a gallery dedicated to him. Bukovac spent most of his years abroad: studying in Paris, visiting England and painting portraits of various aristocrats, and later becoming a professor at the Academy of Art in Prague. However, from time to time he returned to Cavtat, and used this late 18th-century stone building as an atelier. In 1964 it was converted into a gallery displaying a collection of his paintings, drawings, furniture and mementoes.

**Račić Mausoleum** ① *Rat Peninsula, T020-478646, by appointment only, enquire at the Vlaho Bukovac Gallery.* This impressive white stone mausoleum, designed by sculptor Ivan Meštrović in 1921, stands on the highest point of the town cemetery, on Rat Peninsula. An octagonal structure with a cupola, it is made of white stone from the island of Brač. The entrance features a pair of art nouveau-style caryatids (statues of female figures, used as columns to support the porch) and impressive bronze doors. The interior is decorated with reliefs of angels and birds in scenes symbolizing the three stages of life: birth, fate and death. Meštrović built the mausoleum to keep his promise to Marija Račić (a member of a family of wealthy ship owners), who was rumoured to have been his lover. The bronze bell, hanging from the cupola, is inscribed with a touching epitaph, "Know the mystery of love and thou shalt solve the mystery of death and believe that life is eternal."

# Elafiti islands → *For listings, see pages 45-54.*

The tiny Elafiti islands – Koločep, Lopud and Šipan – offer unspoilt nature just a short ferry ride away from Dubrovnik. Pinewoods and scented shrubs cover the islands – the natural vegetation has been largely untouched, apart from on the inland area of Šipan, where there are cultivated fields of grape vines and olive trees. Being car free, the pace of life here is relaxed. Through summer, all three islands offer a number of small hotels and a modest choice of no-frills fish restaurants.

## Koločep

Some 7 km northwest of Gruž harbour, Koločep, with a population of around 150, is the smallest of the inhabited Elafiti islands. There are two settlements: the port of Donje Čelo on the northwest coast and Gornje Čelo on the southeast side; they are linked by a pleasant footpath, shaded by pine trees. The best beach, overlooked by a modern hotel in Donje Čelo, is sandy; there are also secluded pebble beaches, some given over to nudism. Historically the islanders lived from diving for coral, exploiting the nearby reef of Sv Andrija.

## Lopud

The island of Lopud is 12 km northwest of Gruž and is 4.5 km long and 2 km wide. The sole village, also called Lopud, is made up of old stone houses built around the edge of a wide northwest-facing bay, with a view of Sudjuradj on Šipun across the water.

Guarding the entrance to the harbour, on the north side of the bay, stands a semi-derelict 15th-century Franciscan monastery, which was fortified to provide a place of refuge for the entire population in the case of a Turkish attack, and is now under restoration (still to be completed). Close by, the abandoned and roofless Rector's Palace is easily recognized by its fine triple Gothic windows. In stark contrast, on the south side of the bay stands the colossal Lafodia Hotel complex, erected in the 1980s. From Lopud a footpath (15-minute walking time) leads across the island, passing through lush vegetation scented with sage and rosemary to Šunj, a south-facing cove with a generous stretch of sand beach and a couple of summer restaurants.

Most summers (usually in early September), the **Thyssen-Bornemisza Art Contemporary** ① *www.tba21.org*, holds a four-day symposium on Lopud, with seminars dedicated to contemporary art and architecture.

## Šipan

Šipan, the largest of the Elafiti islands, is 9 km long with a width of just over 2.5 km. The main settlements, Šipanska Luka (on the northwest coast) and Sudjuradj (on the southeast coast), are both built at the end of deep narrow inlets and account for a total population of around 500. Šipanska Luka has a palm-lined seafront overlooked by old stone buildings and a hotel – there is a decent beach a short distance from the centre. Sudjuradj is a sleepy fishing village with several small Renaissance villas and a pair of 16th-century watchtowers set back from the harbour, plus the island's second hotel. The two villages lie at opposite ends of Šipansko Polje, a fertile valley planted with olive trees and grape vines, and are connected by a 5-km asphalt road and a network of hiking paths.

## Pelješac Peninsula → *For listings, see pages 45-54.*

Beginning 46 km northwest of Dubrovnik, this long, skinny mountainous peninsula stretches almost 90 km from end to end. High above the coast, a single road runs its entire length, linking a succession of pretty hamlets and offering fine views out over the sea and nearby islands. In the past, fear of pirates meant that most settlements developed on the south-facing slopes, and it was only from the 18th century onwards that any sizeable villages grew up along the coast. Today, its relative lack of development and isolation from the mainland give Pelješac something of an island identity, and most Croatians know it purely for its red wines – Postup and Dingač. Both are truly excellent and can be tasted at several vineyards, which open their cellars to the public throughout the summer. Pelješac's main settlements are Ston and Orebić, both by the sea.

### Arriving on the Pelješac Peninsula

**Getting there**   A regular ferry plies the narrow sea channel between Orebić on Pelješac Peninsula to Dominče on the island of Korčula.

**Tourist information**   **Ston tourist office** ① *Pelješki put 1, Veli Ston, T020-754452, www. ston.hr (summer only).* **Orebić tourist office** ① *Zrinsko-frankopanska 2, T020-713718, www. visitorebic-croatia.hr.*

### Ston

① *Ston fortifications, Jun-Jul 0800-1930, Apr-May and Aug-Sep 0800-1830, Oct 0800-1730, Nov-Mar 1000-1500, 30Kn.*

Some 8 km along Pelješac Peninsula, the fortified village of Ston is made up of two towns, Veli Ston and Mali Ston. It was founded when Dubrovnik took control of Pelješac in 1333, and soon became the Republic's second most important centre. Lying on opposite sides of the peninsula, each with its own bay, the two towns were originally fortified and connected by 5.5 km of defensive walls and 40 towers, effectively controlling land access onto Pelješac. Today the complex is on the UNESCO World Heritage 'Tentative List'. Most visitors come to Ston especially to eat at one of several excellent (but expensive) seafood restaurants.

Veli Ston, on the south side of the peninsula, is made up of Gothic and Renaissance buildings from the 14th and 15th centuries. Below town lies an expanse of saltpans, which once covered more than 400 sq km and provided the Republic of Dubrovnik with one-third of its annual revenue.

The smaller town of Mali Ston, 1 km northeast of Veli Ston, on the north side of the peninsula, can be reached in 15 minutes on foot, following the walls. It's known throughout Croatia for oysters (February-May) and mussels (May-September), which are farmed in the channel of Malostonski Zaljev, between the mainland and the peninsula. The mix of freshwater (from the River Neretva) and saltwater is ideal for cultivating shellfish.

### Orebić

① *Close to the western tip of Pelješac Peninsula and 67 km northwest of Ston.*

Orebić is now Pelješac's top resort, thanks to its fine south-facing beaches and attractive seafront. In the past, it produced many able sea captains, and when they retired they built villas here, which you can still see today. The town is protected from the bura wind by the heights of Sv Ilija Hill (961 m), whose south-facing slopes are dotted with pinewoods, cypresses and agaves. From here it's just 2 km across the Pelješac Channel to the island of

## Pelješac's top vineyards and wine cellars

**Podrum Bartulovića** ① *Prizdrina, T020-742346*. On the road between Ston and Orebić, the Bartulovič family cellar offers wine tasting accompanied by platters of *pršut* (ham), *sir* (cheese) and *slane srdele* (salt sardines), in a beautifully restored traditional konoba.

**Matuško Vina** ① *Potomje, T020-742393*. Approached through a tunnel, the village of Potomje is the true home to the Dingač vineyards. Here, the Matuško family offer wine tasting and also have a shop selling reds from Pelješac and whites from Korčula.

**Grgić** ① *Trstenik, T020-714244*. On a promontory, at the mouth of the tiny port of Trstenik, stands the Grgić winery. Miljenko Grgić, who made his name with the exclusive Grgich Hills Estate, grgich. com, vineyards in California, returned to his Croatian roots in the 1990s to open this winery. Call first to taste white Pošip and red Plavac Mali.

Korčula: the two coasts are linked by a ferry service, making it possible for the people of Orebić to pop to Korčula for an evening out.

Orebić makes a good base for wine tasting (see What to do, page 53) at Pelješac's highly esteemed vineyards, and for windsurfing (see What to do, page 53) at the nearby village of Viganj.

### Franjevački Samostan

① *2 km west of Orebić, T020-713075, Apr-Oct Mon-Sat 0900-1200 and 1600-2000, 20Kn, winter on request.*

A pleasant walk up a winding road lined with cypress trees brings you to the charming Gothic-Renaissance Franciscan Monastery, perched on a craggy cliff 152 m above the sea. It was built in the late 15th century by Franciscan monks, who chose this site for its vista onto the sea channel and surrounding islands. At that time nearby Korčula was under Dubrovnik's arch-rival, Venice. The monks constructed a loggia and terrace, which they used as a vantage point to spy on Venetian galleys; at the first sign of trouble they would send a warning to Dubrovnik by mounted messenger. 'Friendly' ships would let out three blasts of the siren as they passed below the monastery, to which the Franciscans would reply with a peal of the church bells. Inside the monastery you can see a fine collection of religious paintings, notably the *Our Lady of the Angels*, a Byzantine icon apparently washed up by the sea and said to protect sailors from shipwreck. There are also 20 or so votive paintings dedicated to the icon, commissioned by local seamen who survived danger on the ocean.

### Beaches

A 15-minute walk east of Orebić, **Trstenica** is a 1500-m stretch of pebble and sand beach, equipped with sunloungers, parasols, showers and a beach bar and disco (see page 51) through summer. There is also a nearby nudist beach called **Ostupa**.

## Island of Korčula → *For listings, see pages 45-54.*

This long, thin island is green and hilly, with a rocky, indented coastline. It was once covered with dense pine forest, leading the ancient Greeks to call it *Kerkyra Melaina* (Black Corfu). It seems the early Greek settlers lived in relative peace with the local Illyrian tribes, neither attempting to conquer nor assimilate them, but sharing land rights with them, as recorded by a stone inscription from the fourth century BC found in Lumbarda.

Between the 10th and 18th centuries the island came under Venice several times, and with arch-rivals the Republic of Dubrovnik and the Ottoman Empire in close proximity, La Serenissima did all it could to fortify and defend its main base here, the tiny yet culturally advanced Korčula Town. Legendary Venetian explorer, Marco Polo, is believed to have been born in Korčula Town, and an old stone building open to the public is said to have been his family home. Other attractions include evening performances of the Moreška (a medieval sword dance) and excellent local white wines (Grk from Lumbarda and Pošip from the inland villages of Smokvica and Čara).

### Arriving on the island of Korčula

**Getting there** A regular Jadrolinija car ferry plies the narrow sea channel between Orebić on Pelješac Peninsula and Dominče (2 km from Korčula Town) on Korčula, while Mediteranska Plovidba operate another ferry (foot-passengers only) from Orebić direct to Korčula Town. The catamaran Krilo makes daily runs from Split (Central Dalmatia) to Korčula Town. In addition, **Jadrolinija** ① *www.jadrolinija.hr*, runs a coastal ferry several times weekly from Dubrovnik to Rijeka (Kvarner), stopping at the island of Korčula en route. Jadrolinija also runs a daily catamaran from Lastovo to Split (Central Dalmatia), stopping at Vela Luka (on Korčula's west coast) en route.

**Tourist information** Korčula Town tourist office ① *Obala Dr Franje Tudjmana 4, T020-715701, www.visitkorcula.net.*

### Korčula Town

On the island's northeast coast, medieval Korčula Town is a compact cluster of terracotta-roofed houses perched graciously above the sea on a tiny peninsula fortified with walls and round towers. It is on the UNESCO World Heritage 'Tentative List'. The town is backed by hills covered with pinewoods, and faces onto a narrow sea channel offering views of the tall mountainous peaks of Pelješac in the distance. Large, modern hotels have been built a short distance from the centre, leaving the historic core as an open-air museum and making Korčula one of the most popular resorts on the islands, second only to Hvar.

**Kopnena Vrata** The Land Gate is the principal entrance to the old town. A sweeping flight of steps leads up to the 15th-century Revelin Tower, a crenellated quadrangular structure forming an arched gateway into the historic centre. The tower houses a small museum to the Moreška sword dance (see box, opposite) with unpredictable opening hours.

From here, Korčulanskog Statuta runs the length of the tiny peninsula, with narrow streets branching off at odd angles to form a herring-bone pattern, ingeniously preventing local winds from blowing through the heart of town. Through summer, the Moreška sword dance is performed in a walled garden to the left of the Land Gate.

## Moreška

The Moreška (from *morisco*, meaning 'Moorish' in Spanish) came to Korčula via Italy in the 16th century. It originated in Spain in the 12th century, where it was inspired by the struggle of Spanish Christians against the Moors; on the East Adriatic, it was simply adapted to represent the ongoing fight of local Christians against the Turks.

Over the centuries the text, music and pattern of the dance have been altered and shortened, but the central story remains: Bula, a beautiful Muslim maiden, has been kidnapped by the Black Knight, and her sweetheart, the White Knight, comes to her rescue. The performance begins with the Black Knight (dressed in black) dragging Bula in chains, and the maiden crying out against his amorous proposals. The White Knight (confusingly, dressed in red) and his army then arrive, as do the Black Knight's army, ready to defend their leader. The two Knights hurl insults at one another, then cross their swords, and the dance begins. Their armies are pulled into the confrontation, with soldiers clashing swords in pairs within a circle, to the accompaniment of a brass band. The pace of the music gradually accelerates (in the past, performers were often wounded and had to replaced by reserves during the dance), with the black soldiers facing outwards and the circle contracting as they retreat inwards from the white army. Finally, all the black soldiers fall to the ground, the Black Knight surrenders, and the White Knight frees Bula from her chains and kisses her.

In the past, various versions of the dance were found throughout the Mediterranean, where they were probably used as much as an exercise for swordsmen as for entertainment. It also reached Northern Europe, and could well be the forerunner to English Morris dancing, where wooden poles are used instead of swords.

**Katedrala Sv Marka** ① *Strossmayerov Trg, May-Sep Mon-Sat 0900-1900, winter by appointment, 15Kn.* Built of warm yellow-grey stone, Korčula's much-admired Gothic-Renaissance Cathedral of St Mark opens onto Strossmayerov Trg, the main square, in the heart of the old town. The magnificent Romanesque portal is flanked by finely carved figures of Adam and Eve and topped with a statue of St Mark.

Inside, above the main altar stands a 15th-century ciborium (a canopy supported by four columns), carved by the local stonemason Marko Andrijic, who introduced the Renaissance style to the city. Beneath the ciborium, on the main altar, a 19th-century gilt sarcophagus holds the relics of St Theodore (the city's protector) brought to Korčula in 1736. Above it, the painting *St Mark with St Bartholomew and St Jerome* is an early work by the Venetian Mannerist, Tintoretto (1518-1594).

In the southern nave you'll find a curious collection of cannon balls and gruesome-looking weapons used against the Ottoman Turks. Above them, set in a gold frame, hangs a 13th-century icon, *Our Lady with the Child*, formerly kept in the Franciscan church on the island of Badija. When a Turkish fleet, commanded by the Algerian viceroy Uluz-Ali, attacked the town on 15 August 1571, children and the elderly prayed to the icon for divine intervention. Miraculously, a ferocious storm broke, destroying several galleys and causing others to retreat. Also in the southern nave is an *Annunciation* attributed to Tintoretto, while in the apse, a painting above the altar depicting the *Holy Trinity* is the work of another Venetian artist, Leandro Bassano (1557-1622).

# Marco Polo

At the age of 17, Marco Polo (1254-1324), accompanied by his father and uncle, both of whom were Venetian merchants, travelled overland to China along the Silk Route, passing through the mountains and deserts of Persia, and then across the Gobi desert, to arrive, three years later, at the court of the great Mongol Emperor Kublai Khan.

Polo entered the Emperor's diplomatic service, acting as his agent on missions to many parts of the Mongolian Empire for the next 17 years, visiting, or at least gaining extensive knowledge about, Siam (present-day Thailand), Japan, Java, Cochin China (now part of Vietnam), Ceylon (present-day Sri Lanka), Tibet, India and Burma (present-day Myanmar). Some 24 years after their journey began, the Polos returned to Venice, laden with jewels, gold and silk, and eager to recount the extraordinary tales of what they had seen.

In 1298, as a captain in the Venetian fleet, Marco was taken prisoner during a sea battle against the Genoese close to Lumbarda, off the island of Korčula. During a year in prison in Genoa, he dictated the memoirs of his magnificent journeys to a fellow prisoner and romantic novelist, Rusticello of Pisa. Thus his tales of the exotic landscapes and highly refined lifestyles of the Orient first arrived in medieval Europe through *The Travels of Marco Polo*, a best-selling travelogue of its time, which later inspired Christopher Columbus and Vasco da Gama in their voyages of discovery.

**Opatska Riznica** ① *Strossmayerov Trg, May-Sep Mon-Sat 0900-1900, winter by appointment, 25Kn.* Next door to the cathedral, on the first floor of the 17th-century Renaissance-baroque Bishop's Palace, is the Abbey Treasury. Besides an impressive collection of icons and religious paintings, you'll see gold and silver chalices, mass vestments (garments worn by the clergy), ancient coins and a necklace donated to Korčula by Mother Theresa, which had been given to her by the town of Calcutta when she won the Nobel Peace prize in 1979.

**Gradski Muzej** ① *Strossmayerov Trg, T020-711420, Jul-Sep Mon-Sat 1000-2100, Oct-Jun Mon-Sat 1000-1300, 15Kn.* Opposite the cathedral, the 16th-century Renaissance Gabrielis Palace now houses the Town Museum. Exhibits include a copy of the fourth-century BC Greek Lumbardska Psefizma (see box, above), Roman ceramics and a section devoted to local shipbuilding. The building's interior gives some idea of how aristocrats lived between the 16th and 17th centuries, and on the top floor the kitchen is replete with pots and cookery utensils.

**Kuća Marca Pola** ① *Marca Pola bb, Jul-Aug daily 0900-2100, Apr-Jun and Sep-Oct daily 0900-1500, Nov-Mar closed, 20Kn.* Northeast of the main square, behind the cathedral, stands the modest home and watchtower of the Depolo family, now known as the Marco Polo House. Local myth has it that Marco Polo, the legendary 13th-century traveller, was born here, though the present building was constructed several hundred years after his death. It's an amusing enough oddity, however.

**Galerija Ikona** ① *Trg Svih Svetih, T020-711306, Jun-Sep Mon-Sat 0900-1400 and 1700-1800, 15Kn.* Tucked away in a side street in the southeast part of the old town, the Icon Museum contains a display of Cretan School icons painted between the 14th and 17th centuries.

## Lumbardska Psefizma

The Lumbardska Psefizma, a fourth-century BC inscription carved in stone, was found in Lumbarda. Proof of early Greek settlement on this site, it records a decree regarding land distribution, and includes the names of Greek and Illyrian families living here at the time. Today the original is in the Archaeological Museum in Zagreb, but you can see a copy at the Town Museum in Korčula Town.

They arrived in Korčula during the Candian Wars (1645-1669), when the town sent a galley to aid the Venetian fleet in its unsuccessful battle against the Turks for the possession of the Greek island of Crete.

**Beaches** The main town beach is east of the centre, in front of Hotel Marco Polo. However, it gets very busy, so you're better off catching a taxi boat from the harbour to one of the nearby islets, or heading for the neighbouring village of Lumbarda (see below).

### Lumbarda

Some 6 km southeast of Korčula Town, at the eastern tip of the island, the tiny village of Lumbarda is best known for its sandy beach and surrounding vineyards, which produce a dry white wine, Grk. Today, a narrow road lined with mulberry trees leads from the village through vineyards planted with Grk vines, which some experts consider indigenous to Dalmatia, while others, due to its name, conclude that it must have arrived here during ancient times from Greece. Whatever its origin, it grows particularly well in the area's fine reddish sandy soil.

There's little of cultural interest in Lumbarda, though the village itself is a pleasant enough place, strung around a north-facing bay, lined with fish restaurants, cafés and rooms to let. Roads through the vineyards lead to several small beaches. The island's most popular bathing spot is the south-facing sand beach of **Pržina**, backed by a fast-food kiosk and bar, 2 km south of Lumbarda. A short distance east of Lumbarda, the north-facing beach of **Bili Žal** is made up of white stones beaten smooth by the water. A short distance east of Bili Žal is a rocky stretch reserved for nudists.

## Island of Mljet → *For listings, see pages 45-54.*

Mljet, the southernmost of the Croatian islands, is made up of steep rocky slopes and dense pine forests. The western third is a national park and within it is one of the country's most photographed sights: a proud but lonely 12th-century monastery perched on a small island in the middle of an emerald saltwater lake. Through the passing of the centuries, Mljet has remained something of a backwater. No great towns ever grew up here, and today it is home to half a dozen small villages, linked by a single road running the length of the island. Depopulation is a serious problem; the number of people living here has halved over the last 50 years. However, each summer Mljet is rediscovered by a steady flow of nature lovers, discerning travellers and escapists – in recent years visitors include Prince Charles and Steven Spielberg. The island isn't geared towards tourism – most arrive on organized day trips from Dubrovnik, and few remain overnight – but its natural beauty and lack of commercial development make it a wonderful escape for those in search of peace and tranquillity.

### Arriving on the island of Mljet
**Getting there** Jadrolinija ① *www.jadrolinija.hr*, runs a ferry from Dubrovnik to Sobra port on Mljet. **G&V Line** ① *www.gv-line.hr*, covers the same route by catamaran, stopping at the Elafiti islands en route.

**Tourist information** The **tourist office** ① *Polače, T020-744186, www.mljet.hr.*

### Mljet National Park
① *Pristanište, T020-744041, www.np-mljet.hr, the 90Kn entry fee is payable at one of a number of wooden kiosks within the park; if you stay overnight the fee is included in the price of your accommodation.*
In 1960, the western third of the island was declared a national park to protect the indigenous forest of Aleppo pines and holm oaks, and the two magnificent interconnected saltwater lakes, **Malo Jezero** (Little Lake) and **Veliko Jezero** (Big Lake).

The park is ideal for those who enjoy walking or mountain biking: a network of paths criss-cross their way through the forests, and a 9-km trail runs around the perimeter of the two lakes. Southeast of Veliko Jezero, a steep, winding path leads to the highest point within the park, **Montokuc** (253 m), offering stunning views. For swimming, the best bathing areas are on **Solominji Rat**, just south of Mali Most, the bridge over the channel that connects the two lakes. The lakes offer an extended bathing season, the temperature of the water being 4°C warmer than that of the open sea.

You might also wish to take a taxi-boat from Pristanište to Otičić Svete Marije (St Mary's islet), to visit the church and cloister of the Benedictine monastery (no longer in use), which rises in the middle of Veliko Jezero.

It's possible to stay overnight within the park. The island's only hotel, the modern **Hotel Odisej** (see Where to stay, page 47) overlooks Pomena Bay, just a 15-minute walk from Malo Jezero. Alternatively, enquire at the tourist office for private accommodation and rooms to rent.

## Saplunara

On Mljet's southeast tip, Saplunara (from the Latin *sabalum* meaning 'sand') is a protected cove with South Dalmatia's most spectacular sand beach. Close by, in a small, scattered settlement of the same name, several families let rooms and apartments throughout the summer (see Where to stay, page 47). There is also a handful of down-to-earth seasonal fish restaurants. A 20-minute walk from Saplunara, **Blace**, a 1-km long stretch of sand, faces south onto the open sea and backed by pines, is popular with nudists.

## Island of Lastovo → *For listings, see pages 45-54.*

Lastovo is Croatia's second most isolated inhabited island (after Vis). Because of its remoteness it was chosen, like Vis, as a Yugoslav military base, and therefore closed to foreigners from 1976 to 1989. Fortunately this blocked all commercial tourist development and today it is undoubtedly one of the most unspoilt islands on the Adriatic, with dense pinewoods punctuated by meticulously cultivated farmland, an indented coastline with several sheltered bays, and only one true settlement, the charming semi-abandoned Lastovo Town, made up of old stone houses built prior to the turn of the 20th century.

Today, despite a serious problem of depopulation, life goes on. If you visit in spring you'll see a veritable troop of elderly women (plus the occasional donkey) hard at work in the fields. Lastovo is self-sufficient in fruit and vegetables even though only 35% of potential farmland is currently under cultivation. A network of footpaths criss-cross the island, passing through fields, woods and lush vegetation scented with sage, rosemary and mint, making walking a pleasurable pursuit. The islanders will assure you that there are no poisonous snakes – according to local myth, several centuries ago a priest saw an adder here and cursed it, after which all the island's snakes threw themselves into the sea.

### Arriving on the island of Lastovo

**Getting there**   The main ferry port is in Ubli. **Jadrolinija** ⓘ *www.jadrolinija.hr*, runs a daily ferry and fast catamaran from Lastovo to Split (Central Dalmatia), stopping at Vela Luka (island of Korčula) and Hvar Town (island of Hvar) en route.

**Tourist information**   Lastovo Town tourist office ⓘ *Pjevor bb, T020-801018, tz-lastovo.hr*, is opposite the bus stop on the hill above Lastovo Town.

### Lastovo Town

Ten kilometres northeast of Ubli (the port) and 1 km inland from the north coast, Lastovo Town stands 86 m above sea level. This once-wealthy community is made up of closely packed old stone houses, built into a south-facing slope, forming an amphitheatre-like space focusing on carefully tended allotment gardens in the fertile valley below. The buildings date from the 15th century onwards and are noted for their unusual chimneys, which are strangely similar to minarets. A series of steep, cobbled paths wind their way between the houses, and to the east side of town stand the 15th-century parish church of Sv Kuzme i Sv Damjana (St Cossimo and St Damian) and a pretty open-sided loggia. Above town, perched on a triangular hill known as Glavica, is Kaštel, a fortress erected by the French in 1810 and now used as a meteorological station. It's worth the climb up for its breathtaking views.

## Ubli

The island's main ferry port, Ubli is a curious cluster of modern buildings. Founded by Mussolini as a fishing village in 1936, when the island was under Italy, it was initially populated with fishermen from Istria. However, after just one year they packed up and left, so Il Duce sent a community of Italians from the island of Ponza, instead. There's nothing much to see, but from here a pleasant 3-km coastal road leads to **Uvala Pasadur** (Pasadur Bay), where you'll find Lastovo's only hotel.

## Beaches

Through summer, locals transport visitors by boat to the Lastovčici (an archipelago of over 40 islets lying northeast of Lastovo) usually stopping at the tiny uninhabited island of Saplun where there's a secluded cove with a blissful sand beach.

# Dubrovnik and South Dalmatian Coast listings

*For hotel and restaurant price codes and other relevant information, see pages 12-19.*

## ⊜ Where to stay

### Dubrovnik *p26, maps p26 and p30*
**Old Town**
**€€€€ Pučić Palace**, Ulica od Puca 1, T020-326000, www.thepucicpalace.com. Overlooking the open-air market, this luxurious boutique hotel is the most romantic (and expensive) place to stay in Dubrovnik's old town. Occupying a restored 18th-century baroque palace, its 19 rooms are furnished with antiques and have extras such as Italian mosaic-tiled bathrooms stocked with Bulgari toiletries. If you're going to splash out for just one night, this could be the place to do it.
**€€€ Stari Grad Hotel**, Od Sigurate 4, T020-322244, www.hotelstarigrad.com. One of only 2 hotels within the city walls, this old stone building is close to Pile Gate, just off Placa. Inside there are 8 guest rooms furnished with reproduction antiques, and a roof terrace where breakfast is served throughout summer. Under new management, it was renovated in winter 2012.
**€€ Amoret Apartments**, Dinka Ranjine ulica, Old Town, T020-324005, www.dubrovnik-amoret.com. Occupying 3 17th-century stone buildings in the old town, **Amoret** has 15 doubles rooms, each with wooden parquet flooring and antique furniture, free Wi-Fi, and a kitchenette so you can cook. The owner, Branka Dabrović, is extremely kind and helpful, and full of local advice.
**€€ Karmen Apartments**, Bandureva 1, T020-323433, www.karmendu.com. For a quaint hideaway in the old town, try this delightful little guesthouse run by the Van Bloemen family, who also own the **Hard Jazz Café Trubador**. The 4 light and airy apartments have wooden floors, colourful painted wooden furniture and

handmade bedspreads, and offer views onto the old harbour. The entrance is down a narrow side street between the Rector's Palace and the Aquarium.
**€ Fresh Sheets Hostel**, Sv Simuna 15, T091 7992086, www.freshsheetshostel.com. This friendly hostel is run by a Canadian-Croatian couple, and offers 4-bed and 8-bed dorms, plus a private double room with sea views. There's a kitchen area in reception, where guests have a do-it-yourself breakfast.

**Outside the Old Town**
**€€€ Hotel Bellevue**, Pera Cingrije 7, T020-330000, www.hotel-bellevue.hr. Built into a cliff face overlooking the sea, halfway between the old town and Lapad Peninsula, this chic hotel reopened in autumn 2006 following total renovation. The 81 rooms are furnished in smart minimalist style with wooden floors, and the 12 suites also have jacuzzis. Facilities include a small beach and a luxurious spa and wellness centre.
**€€€ Hotel Lapad**, Lapadska obala 37, T020-455555, www.hotel-lapad.hr. On Lapad Peninsula, overlooking Gruž harbour, this four-star hotel was refurbished in 2008. It has 157 rooms and 6 suites, with modern minimalist furniture and fabrics in earthy shades of brown, beige and cream, plus slick tiled bathrooms with glass doors so the bedroom is visible. There's an outdoor pool in the garden.
**€€ Berkeley Hotel**, Andrije Hebranga 116A, T020-494160, www.berkeleyhotel.hr. Overlooking Gruž harbour, the Berkeley is run by a welcoming Croatian family who lived for many years in Sydney, Australia. There are 16 spacious suites and studios (with kitchenettes), plus 8 double rooms, all with wooden floors, slick minimalist furnishing, flat-screen satellite TV and internet. There's a new outdoor pool, they do an excellent cooked-to-order breakfast, and their 'Stay and Cruise' offer combines

several nights at the hotel with a few days exploring the Elafiti islands by motorboat.

**€€ MirO Studio Apartments**, Svetoga Đurđa 16, T099-4242442, www.mirostudio apartmentsdubrovnik.com. Just outside the Old Town, close to Pile Gate, MirO offers 7 smart 2-person apartments, each with a kitchenette, modern minimalist décor, and free Wi-Fi.

## Cavtat *p33*
**€€ Hotel Supetar**, Dr Ante Starčevića 27, T020-479833, www.adriaticluxuryhotels. com. In an old stone building set back a little from the seafront, this basic but welcoming hotel has 28 rooms (sea view and garden view), and a restaurant and waterside summer terrace.

**€€ Hotel Villa Pattiera**, Trumbićev put 9, T020-478800, www.villa-pattiera.hr. On the seafront promenade in the centre of Cavtat, this old stone villa has been refurbished to form a delightful, family-run boutique hotel. There are 12 rooms, all with wooden floors and either a sea or garden view. Breakfast is served in the popular **Restaurant Dalmacija** on the ground floor.

## Elafiti islands *p35*
### Lopud
**€€ La Villa**, Iva Kuljevana 33, Lopud, T091-322 0126, www.lavilla.com.hr. In a 19th-century villa overlooking Lopud Bay, this small, reasonably priced hotel is run by a young, friendly Croatian couple. The 8 guest rooms have IKEA-style minimalist modern furniture and coloured Indian fabrics, mosaic-tile bathrooms, and they either look out onto the open sea or the back garden's giant magnolia tree, orange trees and lavender bushes. You get breakfast in the garden, and dinner on request.

**€€ Villa Vilina**, Obala Iva Kuljevana 5, Lopud, T020-759333, www.villa-vilina.hr. Occupying a restored stone villa set in a garden with a terrace overlooking the sea, this hotel has 15 rooms and suites, an excellent restaurant and a small outdoor

pool. It is located just in front of the ferry landing station.

## Šipan
**€€ Hotel Božica**, Sudjuradj 13, Šipan, T020-325400, www.hotel-bozica.hr. In Sudjuradj, 5 km from the port of Šipanska Luka, this hotel has 22 rooms and 4 suites, all with wooden floors, simple modern furnishing, internet, minibar and satellite TV, and most with a balcony. There's a restaurant with a terrace, an outdoor pool and a pier where yachts can moor.

**€€ Hotel Šipan**, Šipanska Luka 160, Šipan, T020-754900, www.hotel-sipan.hr. This 3-storey white building is on the edge of town, overlooking the palm-lined seafront promenade. There are 85 slick, modern rooms furnished in minimalist style, a bar and a waterside restaurant with big white parasols. One-day fishing trips and massage can be arranged upon request.

## Pelješac Peninsula *p36*
### Ston
**€€ Hotel Ostrea**, Mali Ston, T020-754555, www.ostrea.hr. This former mill has been restored to form a small luxury hotel, with 9 rooms and 1 suite, all with parquet flooring and antique furniture. Through summer, breakfast is served on a pleasant open-air terrace.

### Orebić
**€€ Boutique Hotel Adriatic**, Šetalište Kneza Domagoja 8, T020-714488, www. hoteladriaticorebic.com. In a restored 17th-century stone villa on the coast, close to the ferry landing station, this boutique hotel has 6 rooms, the best ones with sea views. The staff are friendly and helpful, and there's a reliable ground floor restaurant, **Stari Kapetan** (see page 50), where a breakfast is served, with outside tables through summer.

**€€ Hotel Indijan**, Škvar 2, Orebić, T020-714555, www.hotelindijan.hr. This classy, family-run hotel, which opened in 2007, overlooks the beach in the centre of Orebić. Combining traditional and modern architecture, it has 17 rooms and 2 suites, with pale wood furniture and wooden floors. Facilities include a restaurant with a palm-lined terrace, a lounge bar, an indoor pool and a sauna.

## Island of Korčula *p38*
### Korčula Town
**€€€€ Lešić Dimitri Palace**, Don Pavla Pose 1-6, T020-715560, www.lesic-dimitri. com. In the old town, this cluster of medieval stone buildings has been lovingly resorted to create an incredibly luxurious 'apartotel' with chic modern furnishing and quirky details such as open-plan bedrooms with free-standing bathtubs. There are 5 'residences' (sleeping 2-7), all with sleek kitchenettes, plus a gourmet restaurant, a small spa with Thai masseurs and 2 hotel yachts.
**€€ Hotel Korsal**, Šetalište Frana Kršinića 80, T020-715722, www.hotel-korsal.com. Opened in 2010, this family-run hotel lies a 10-min walk from the centre, with a small pebble beach nearby and views of the old town fortifications across the bay. It has ten modern rooms, all with sea views and bathrooms with under floor heating, plus a waterside restaurant where breakfast is served.

### Lumbarda
**€ Apartmani Val**, Uvala Račišće bb, T020-712430, www.korcula-val.com. A 20-min walk from Lumbarda, in a garden overlooking the peaceful Račišč Bay, Val has 3 apartments, each with a sea-view terrace and Wi-Fi. The host, a retired-chef, prepares delicious fresh seafood suppers on request. He also has bikes and a small boat to hire, and will collect you by car if you are arriving through Korčula Town. Great hospitality.
**€ Hotel Lumbarda**, Lumbarda bb, T020-712700, www.lumbardahotel.com. This modern hotel overlooks the sea and has 44 smallish but comfortable rooms, each with an en suite bathroom and a balcony, most with sea views. There's a small outdoor pool and a scuba-diving club. It's a 10-min walk to the beach, and the bus to Korčula Town stops outside the hotel.

## Island of Mljet *p42*
**€€ Hotel Odisej**, Pomena, T020-362111, www.adriaticluxuryhotels.com. Lying within the national park, a pleasant 15-min walk from Malo Jezero, this cluster of modern white buildings, overlooking Pomena Bay, is Mljet's only hotel. The best of the basic 155 rooms each have a sea-view balcony, a/c, TV and minibar. Facilities include bicycles, surfboards and kayaks to rent, plus a small wellness centre.
**€ Stermasi**, Saplunara 2, Maranovici, T020-746179, www.stermasi.hr. Overlooking the bay, just a short walk from the lovely sand beach of Saplunara, **Stermasi** has 7 simple but comfortable apartments, each with a kitchenette. The owner also runs a rustic konoba (see page 50) serving barbecued fish and meat, and has bikes and small boats to rent.
**€ Villa Mirosa**, Saplunara 26, T020-746133, www.villa-mirosa.com. Close to Saplunara sand beach, **Villa Mirosa** has 6 basic but comfortable rooms, all with a/c and en suite bathrooms. There's a ground-floor restaurant (see page 50) with a lovely, shady terrace, and the owner also offers to take guests on fishing trips.

## Island of Lastovo *p43*
**€€ Hotel Solitudo**, Ulava Pasadur bb, 3 km north of Ubli, T020-802100, www. hotel-solitudo.com. After several years under renovation, this hotel now has 73 rooms all with a/c, satellite TV and en suite bathroom. Backed by pinewoods, it overlooks the sea and tiny island of Prežba, which is linked to Lastovo by a bridge. Facilities include a restaurant, rustic konoba, wellness centre (sauna, jacuzzi and gym) and scuba-diving centre.

€€ **Vila Antica**, Sv Kuzma i Damjana 3, Lastovo Town, T098-447311, www.vila-antica.com. This lovely old stone cottage has 2 double bedrooms, a fully equipped yellow kitchen, a slick modern bathroom and a cosy living room with a beamed ceiling. It was renovated in 2006, and makes a romantic escape both in summer and out of season.

€ **Apartments Madirazza**, Pasadur bb, T021-734085, www.apartmani-lastovo.com. In a modern white building overlooking the sea, this house has 3 self-catering apartments, each with a kitchen, sea-view terrace, a/c and satellite TV. It's 3 km from the port at Ubli.

€ **Triton**, Zaklopatica, T020-801161, www.triton.hr. Above the excellent seafood restaurant of the same name (see page 51), you'll find several basic but comfortable rooms, the best ones with balconies and views over the peaceful bay, which often fills up with sailing boats in the evening.

## 🍴 Restaurants

### Dubrovnik *p26, maps p26 and p30*
### Old Town

€€ **Kamenica**, Gundulićeva Poljana 8, T020-323682. Overlooking the open-air market within the town walls, **Kamenica** is a down-to-earth eatery much loved by locals for its fresh oysters and simple seafood dishes. The platters of *girice* (small fried fish) and *pržene lignje* (fried squid) make a delicious lunchtime snack.

€€ **Lokanda Peškarija**, Na Ponti bb, overlooking the old harbour just outside the city walls, T020-324750, www.mea-culpa.hr. Offering excellent value for money and always busy, this informal seafood eatery stands next to the covered fish market. Indoors there's a split-level, candlelit dining space with exposed stonework and wooden beams, but the best tables are outside with sea views.

€€ **Nishta**, Prijeko bb, 020-322088, www.nishtarestaurant.com. While most restaurants in this pretty stone alley are tourist traps, this welcoming vegetarian eatery is a real find. Cooking with fragrant herbs and spices, it borrows influences from afar to conjure up an eclectic menu, including tasty gazpacho, falafels and burritos. The name, **Nishta** (or ništa), means 'nothing' in Croatian.

€€ **Proto**, Široka 1, in a side street off Stradun, T020-323234, www.esculap restaurants.com. In the old town, up-market Proto offer tables on a lovely vine-covered, upper-level, open-air terrace. The restaurant dates back to 1886 and has an excellent reputation for traditional Dalmatian seafood dishes such as oysters from nearby Ston, and barbecued meats, notably succulent steaks.

€€ **Taj Mahal**, Gučetića 2, T020-323221, www.tajmahaldubrovnik.com. Despite its name, this eatery specializes in Bosnian dishes, not Indian. Come here for barbecued meats such as *čevapi* (rissoles made from minced beef) and *ražnjići* (tiny pieces of pork cooked on a skewer), plus Bosnian favourites *krompiruša* (filo-pastry pies filled with potato) and *zeljanica* (filo-pastry pies filled with spinach and cheese).

€ **Buffet Škola**, Antuninska ulica bb, T020-321096. In a narrow side street between Placa and Prijeko, this family-run sandwich bar is known far beyond Dubrovnik. Sandwiches come in delicious home-made bread, filled with locally produced *sir iz ulja* (cheese in oil), pršut (dried ham) and tomatoes from the villages of Konavle.

€ **Mea Culpa**, Za Rokom 3, T020-323430, www.mea-culpa.hr. Locally recommended for the best (and biggest) pizza in town, plus lasagne and a limited choice of salads, what was once a tiny eatery has expanded over the years, and now occupies a row of 3 buildings. It has long line of tables outside on the cobbled street in summer. Service can be slow when it's busy, but its friendly and fun.

## Outside the Old Town

**€€ Orsan**, Ivana Zajca 2, Lapad Peninsula, T020-436822, www.restaurant-orsan-dubrovnik.com. This waterside eatery has a pleasant, leafy terrace overlooking the small marina in Gruž Harbour, making it popular with yachters. Favourite dishes are *salata od hobotnice* (octopus salad), *svježa morska riba* (fresh fish) and *rozata* (a Dubrovnik dessert similar to crème caramel).

**€€ Taverna Otto**, Nikole Tesle 8, T095-2197608, www.tavernaotto.com. Near Gruž port, in a lovely old stone building overlooking a small harbour, this friendly unpretentious eatery opened in 2012. The menu is short and everything is freshly prepared – try the rump steak with green peppercorn sauce, followed by a divine chocolate soufflé.

**€€ Tovjerna Sesame**, Dante Alighieria bb, in a side street off Dr Ante Starčevića, T020-412910, www.sesame.hr. Just outside the city walls, close to Pile Gate, this romantic eatery is a perfect venue for a light supper over a bottle of good wine. The menu features platters of cheeses and cold meats, truffle dishes and an enticing variety of creative salads.

## Cavtat *p33*

**€€ Konavoski Komin**, Velji Do, Konavle, T020-479607. Out of town, 6 km northeast of Cavtat, this old stone building, with tables on a series of outdoor terraces through summer, serves traditional Dalmatian food and wine. It's possible to reach via the marked Ronald Brown Pathway from Cavtat – allow 1 hr 30 min.

**€€ Leut**, Trumbićev Put 11, T020-478477, www.restaurant-leut.com. In business for over 40 years, this excellent fish restaurant is in the centre of town, with a large summer terrace overlooking the seafront. The house speciality is scampi cream risotto.

## Elafiti islands *p35*
### Lopud

**€€ Konoba Peggy**, Narikla 22, T020-759036. Up a narrow side street above the ferry quay, this informal eatery has a pretty terrace with heavy wooden tables and benches, and fragrant lemon trees. Expect authentic Dalmatian fare, notably fresh fish, which the owner cooks over an open fire.

**€€ Restoran Obala**, Obala Iva Kuljevana bb, Lopud, T020-759170. Local meat and fish specialities served at tables on the seafront promenade, with fantastic sunset views across the bay. They also stage occasional live traditional Dalmatian music.

### Šipan

**€€ Kod Marka**, Šipanska Luka, T020-758007. Overlooking the harbour, with several tables beneath white umbrellas on the waterside terrace out front, this informal eatery serves outstanding local seafood dishes such as *rižot na lučki način* (risotto with lobster, aubergine and courgette) along with more experimental dishes like octopus burgers. Be sure to try the home-made *rakija*.

## Pelješac Peninsula *p36*
### Ston

**€€ Bota Šare**, Mali Ston bb, T020-754482, www.bota-sare.hr. Occupying the 14th-century salt warehouse, this restaurant is recommended for locally grown shellfish. If you have a sweet tooth, round off with the stonski makaruli, a bizarre local pudding made from pasta, nuts, sugar and cinnamon baked in a pastry crust.

**€€ Kapetanova Kuća**, Mali Ston, T020-754264. This highly regarded restaurant draws connoisseurs from all over Croatia. The house speciality is fresh oysters, but there's also a good choice of seafood risotto and pasta dishes, plus fresh fish. It's run by the same family that own the nearby Hotel Ostrea.

## Orebić

**€€ Konoba Antunović**, Kuna, 16 km east of Orebić, T020-742101, www.opgantunovic. hr. In the village of Kuna, in a valley set back from the coast, this authentic agrotourism centre serves home produce at heavy wooden tables and benches in an old stone building with a beamed ceiling. Expect platters of anchovies, olives, pršut and sheep's cheese, plus local stews and freshly baked bread. Be sure to try the house wines, the white rukatac and red plavac mali.

**€€ Stari Kapetan**, Šetalište Kneza Domagoja 8, T020-714488. On the coast, close to the ferry landing station, you'll find this restaurant on the ground floor of **Hotel Adriatic** (see Where to stay, page 46). It does good fresh local seafood, and has outdoor tables on a (slightly kitsch) wooden front terrace, built to look like a boat.

## Island of Korčula p38
## Korčula Town and around

**€€ Adio Mare**, Svetog Roka, T020-711253. In a narrow side street in Korčula old town, close to the Marco Polo House, this memorable restaurant has kept the same down-to-earth menu, including *pašta-fažol* (beans and pasta), *brodet* (fish stew served with polenta) and *paštičada* (beef stewed in prošek and prunes, served with gnocchi), since it opened in 1974. It's outrageously popular so reservations are recommended – in the past it worked dinner only, but is now open for both lunch and dinner.

**€€ Filippi**, Šetalište Petra Kanavelića, T020-711690, www.restaurantfilippi.com. On Korčula's waterside promenade, this sophisticated restaurant opened in summer 2012 and serves creative Dalmatian cuisine. Look out for sublime dishes such as baked octopus on truffle polenta, or red snapper fillet served on black Beluga lentils with okra. A little pricey, but worth it.

**€€ Konoba Marinero**, Ulica Marka Andrijića 13, T020-711170. With wooden tables and benches set out on the stone steps in a narrow side street in Korčula old town, Marinero is run by 2 brothers who are both fishermen. Informal and discreet, it serves the best fresh fish and seafood in the area.

**€€ Konoba Mate**, Pupnat, T020-717109. In the village of Pupnat, a 15-min drive from Korèula Town, this highly regarded agrotourism centre serves delicious home-made ravioli filled with goat's cheese, lamb casserole and seasonal specialities such as wild asparagus omelette. Be sure to round it all off with a glass of homemade *travarica* (rakija flavoured with herbs).

**€€ Pizzeria Tedeschi**, Šetalište Petra Kanavelića, T020-711586. In Korčula old town, with tables lining the seafront promenade, affording views across channel to Orebić, family-run Tedeschi serves the best pizza in town.

**€€ Ranč Maha**, Stiva, Žrnovo, T098-494389. Open weekends only during winter. This small agrotourism centre occupies a stone building set amid fields near the rural village of Žrnovo, and serves authentic home-made food and wine. Peaceful and rustic.

## Lumbarda

**€ Pizzeria Torkul**, Mala Glavica, Lumbarda, T020-712129. With an open-air terrace overlooking the sea, this friendly eatery does delicious thin-base pizzas from a brick oven. Try the Torkul, topped with mozzarella, mushrooms, tomatoes and *pršut* (prosciutto).

## Island of Mljet p42

**€€ Calypso**, Polače 13, T020-744070. Overlooking the bay, with yachts moored up out front, this friendly restaurant is popular with sailing people. Come here for fresh seafood dishes and barbecued fish, or delicious lamb, slow cooked under a peka.

**€€ Marijina Konoba**, Požura, T020-746113. Overlooking the lovely Požura Bay, this family-run gourmet eatery is one of the best places to indulge in fresh seafood such as lobster, as well as locally caught wild boar. The olive oil is their own, and the bread is freshly baked each day.

**€€ Stermasi**, Saplunara 2, Maranovici, T020-746179, www.stermasi.hr. Overlooking the bay, just a short walk from the lovely sand beach of Saplunara, this rustic konoba serves delicious casseroles prepared under a *peka* (try the octopus or goat) and a decent house wine. They also have apartments to rent (see Where to stay, page 47).

**€€ Villa Mirosa**, Saplunara 26, T020-746133, www.villa-mirosa.com. Close to Saplunara sand beach, this rustic restaurant serves freshly caught seafood on a lovely, shady terrace, along with homemade olive oil, wine and *rakija*. The owner also has 6 rooms to rent (see Where to stay, page 47).

### Island of Lastovo *p43*

**€€ Konoba Augusta Insula**, Zaklopatica, T020-801167, www.augustainsula.com. With 3 terraces above the Zaklopatica Bay, this konoba serves up excellent lobster and spaghetti, as well as fresh fish and delicious locally gathered *motar* (rock samphire). They also organize fishing trips, and have several mooring places out front, complete with water and electricity supplies for yachters.

**€€ Konoba Bačvara**, Po* žival bb, Lastovo Town, T020-801131. Open Jun-Oct. Hidden away in an old stone building with a rustic interior in the lower part of Lastovo Town, this traditional konoba serves up fresh seafood, locally produced vegetables and wine.

**€€ Konoba Porto Rosso**, Skrivena Luka, T020-801261, www.portorus.com. With tables set out on a terrace looking out over the 'hidden bay', this eatery attracts yachters, who can moor up outside (18 berths, plus electricity and water supplies) and hop ashore for a meal of fresh seafood and local organic produce.

**€€ Konoba Triton**, Zaklopatica, T020-801161, www.triton.hr. Considered by many to be the best restaurant on the island, Triton is popular with yachters, who moor up directly in front of the summer terrace that has views of Zaklopatica Bay. The owner catches fresh fish daily, and has rooms to rent upstairs (see Where to stay, page 48).

## 🎵 Bars and clubs

**Dubrovnik** *p26, maps p26 and p30*
**Buža**, Od Margarite, T091-589 4936. Accessed through a small doorway in the city walls, looking out to sea, you'll find this informal bar by following the 'Cold Drinks' sign. Tables are arranged on a series of terraces set into the rocks. The drinks in question are served in plastic cups, but the mellow music and night-time candles make it many people's favourite Dubrovnik bar.

**D'Vino**, Palmotićeva 4a, T020-321130, dvino.net. This friendly little wine bar has a fine selection of over 60 local and imported wines, served by the glass, bottle, or as wine 'flights' (selection of 3 wines, either red or white, with description). They also do platters of cheese and/or cured meats. Open daily till 0200.

**Eastwest**, Frana Supila bb, T020-412220, www.ew-dubrovnik.com. In a 1970s modernist building, overlooking the old harbour, during the day this chic club runs a café and a private pebble beach equipped with sunloungers and umbrellas, but come early evening, the cocktail bar and restaurant opend and a party mood sets in. There's a rooftop VIP open-air lounge open until 0500, where you might spot some well-known faces from the world of sport and cinema.

**Hard Jazz Café Trubadour**, Bunićeva Poljana 2, T020-323476. In the old town, this cosy bar is crammed with old furniture, candles, jazz memorabilia and signed photos of well-known people who have been here. It stages occasional live jazz concerts on a small stage outside through summer. It's owned by the Van Bloemen family, who founded London's renowned **Troubadour Café** in Earl's Court in 1954, and moved to Dubrovnik in 1972.

### Pelješac Peninsula *p36*
**Trstenica Club**, Orebić beach, T098-9790501, www.trstenicaclub.com. Beach bar and disco on Orebić's main beach, day and night.

### Island of Korčula *p38*
**Cocktail Bar Massimo**, Šetalište Petra Kanavelića bb, Korčula Town, T020-715073. In the old town fortifications, inside the Tiepolo Tower on the tip of the peninsula, this bar is famed for its splendid sunset views over the sea.

**Tramonto Cocktail Bar**, Šetalište Petra Kanavelića bb, Korčula Town, T020-715401. This family-run cocktail bar serves great drinks on a waterside terrace, also well positioned for spectacular sunsets.

## ❀ Festivals

**Dubrovnik** *p26, maps p26 and p30*
**3 Feb** Sveti Vlaho, each year, Dubrovnik celebrates its patron with the Feast of St Blaise. A ceremonial holy service is held in front of the cathedral at 1000, followed by a religious procession around town at 1130; the remains of St Blaise, in the form of relics, take pride of place. During the time of the republic, those prisoners who did not present a threat to public safety were released on this day to participate in the festivities.
**Feb** Dubrovnik Carnival, a week of festivities in the Old Town, culminating with a masked ball on the final night.
**Jun** Dubrovnik Opera Festival, www.dubrovnik-opera-festival-com. A 4-day celebration of opera, held in the Rector's Palace courtyard.
**Mid-Jul to mid-Aug** Dubrovnik Summer Festival, www.dubrovnik-festival.hr. Each year, this highly acclaimed international festival hosts drama, ballet, concerts and opera at open-air venues within the city walls.

**Cavtat** *p33*
**Sep** Epidaurus Festival, www.epidaurus festival.com. This 10-day international music and art festival stages open-air concerts (classical and jazz) plus exhibitions and theatre.

**Pelješac Peninsula** *p36*
**Late Jul-late Aug** Ston Summer Festival, Ston, www.ston.hr. This summer festival stages open-air evening music and theatre in the centre of Veli Ston, given partial coverage by Croatian television.

### Island of Korčula *p38*
**May-Oct** Moreška, this traditional sword dance is performed at 2100 each Tue and Thu, next to the Land Gate, at the entrance into the old town. Tickets (100Kn), which should be booked in advance, are available from travel agencies and hotel receptions around town.

## ❂ Shopping

**Dubrovnik** *p26, maps p26 and p30*
**Books**
**Algoritam**, Placa 8, T020-322044. The best bookshop for foreign-language publications including novels, travel guides and maps.

**Food and drink**
**Dubrovačka Kuća**, Svetog Dominika bb, near Ploče Gate, T020-322092. Tastefully laid out shop stocking the best Croatian wines, rakija, olive oil and truffle products. There's a gallery upstairs.

**Souvenirs**
**Boutique Croata**, Pred Dvorom 2, T020-638330, www.croata.hr. Sells original Croatian ties in presentation boxes, with a history of the tie.

### Island of Korčula *p38*
**Souvenirs**
**Aromatica**, Ulica Depola 96, Korčula Town, T020-711900, www.aromatica.hr. Delicious-smelling soaps, shampoos and massage oils made from local aromatic herbs.

## 🅞 What to do

**Dubrovnik** *p26, maps p26 and p30*
**Adventure sports**
**Adriatic Kayak Tours**, Zrinsko-franko
panska 6, T020-312770, www.adriatickayak
tours.com. Arranges half-day and full-day
kayaking tours, as well as a 1-day pedal-
and-paddle tour involving kayaking from
Lopud to Šipan then riding a mountain
bike the length of the island.

**Diving**
**Diving Centre Blue Planet**, Hotel Dubrovnik
Palace, Masarykov put 20, T091-899 0973,
www.blueplanet-diving.com.

**Cavtat** *p33*
**Diving**
**Epidaurum Diving and Watersports
Centre**, Šetalište Žal bb, T020-471386,
www.epidaurum.com.

**Pelješac Peninsula** *p36*
**Diving**
**Adriatic**, Mokola 6, Orebić, T020-714328,
www.adriatic-mikulic.com.

**Windsurfing**
**Maritimo**, Ponta, Viganj, T098-9270470,
www.windsurfing-kitesurfing-viganj.com.

**Wine tasting**
**Bartulović Vina**, Prizdrina (13 km
southeast of Orebić), T020-742506,
www.vinarijabartulovic.hr.
**Matuško Vina**, Potomje 5a, Potomje
(15 km southeast of Orebić), T020-742399,
www.matusko-vina.hr.

**Island of Korčula** *p38*
**Boating**
**Cro Rent**, Obala Hrvatskih Mornara bb,
Korčula Town, T020-711908, www.cro-rent.
com. Rents speedboats as well as cars,
mopeds and motorbikes.

**Diving**
**MM Sub**, Lumbarda bb, Lumbarda,
T020-712288, www.mm-sub.hr.

**Island of Mljet** *p42*
**Adventure sports**
**Hotel Odisej**, you can rent mountain bikes,
kayaks and canoes, by the hour or by the
day (see Where to stay, page 47).

**Island of Lastovo** *p43*
**Diving**
**Paradise Diving Centre**, Pasadur bb, Ubli,
T020-805179, www.diving-paradise.net.

## 🅣 Transport

See also Transport in Dubrovnik
and the Dalmatian Coast, page 10.

**Dubrovnik** *p26, maps p26 and p30*
**Bus**
From Dubrovnik, frequent buses run
to **Cavtat** (40 mins), **Ston** (1 hr 40 mins)
and **Orebić** (3 hrs), also to **Split** (4 hrs),
**Zadar** (7½ hrs), **Rijeka** (11 hrs) and
**Zagreb** (9-11 hrs, depending on the route).

**Train**
Dubrovnik is not connected to the rest of
the country by rail.

## 🅞 Directory

**Dubrovnik** *p26, maps p26 and p30*
**Hospital** Roka Mišetića bb, T020-431777.
**Pharmacy** Gruž at Gruška obala, T020-
418990, and Kod Zvonika on Stradun, T020-
321133, alternate as 24-hr pharmacies.

**Cavtat** *p33*
**Pharmacy** Ljekarna Mišković Cavtat,
Trumbićev put 2, T020-478261.

**Orebić**
**Pharmacy** Ljekarna Orebić, Bana Jelačića
bb, Orebić, T020-713019.

**Island of Korčula** *p38*
**Pharmacy** Ljekarna Korčula, Trg Kralja
Tomislava bb, Korčula Town, T020-711057.
**Hospital** The nearest hospital is in
Dubrovnik on the mainland.

**Island of Mljet** *p42*
**Pharmacy** Ljekarna Mljet,
Babino Polje, T020-745005.

**Island of Lastovo** *p43*
**Pharmacy** Ljekarna Split,
Lastovo Town, T020-801276.

## Contents

## Footprint features

Central Dalmatian Coast

## Split → *For listings, see pages 74-85.*

Split is Croatia's second largest city, after Zagreb, and the main point of arrival for visitors to Dalmatia. The old town lies within the walls of Diocletian's Palace – a vast structure commissioned by Roman Emperor Diocletian in AD 295. When the palace was completed in AD 305, Diocletian resigned and retired to his beloved homeland until his death in AD 313.

The palace then lay semi-abandoned until 615, when refugees from Salona – which had been sacked by tribes of Avars and Slavs – found shelter within its sturdy walls, and divided up the imperial apartments into modest living quarters. It thus began to develop into a city in its own right. By the 11th century the settlement had spread beyond the ancient walls, and during the 14th century, an urban conglomeration west of the palace was fortified, thus doubling the city area.

Today it's an extraordinary mix of the old and the new: magnificent ancient buildings, proud baroque palaces, romantic cobbled back streets, a palm-lined seafront promenade with a string of open-air cafés, and a vibrant nightlife. With several well-equipped marinas, it's also Croatia's top base for yacht charter companies, should you wish to explore the region in the best way possible, aboard a sailing boat.

### Arriving in Split
**Getting there** Split Airport ① *T021-203555, www.airport-split.hr*, lies 20 km direction west of the city centre and is served by regular shuttle bus (30Kn). The **bus station** is at ① *Obala Kneza Domagoja 12, T060-327777, www.ak-split.hr*. For regional bus travel, see page 10. The ferry port is immediately in front of the bus and train stations. **Jadrolinija** ① *www.jadrolinija.hr*, and **Blue Line** ① *www.blueline-ferries.com*, both operate overnight

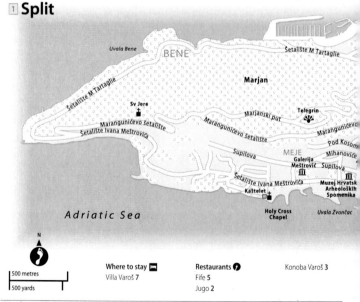

### 1 Split

*Adriatic Sea*

500 metres
500 yards

| Where to stay 🛏 | Restaurants 🍴 | Konoba Varoš **3** |
|---|---|---|
| Villa Varoš **7** | Fife **5** | |
| | Jugo **2** | |

ferries from Split to Ancona in Italy. Through summer, the Italian company **SNAV** ① *www. snav.it*, runs a high-speed catamaran to Ancona. Jadrolinija also runs frequent local ferries and catamarans to the surrounding Dalmatian islands. The **train station** is at ① *Obala Kneza Domagoja 9, T060-333444, www.hznet.hr*.

**Tourist information** There are **tourist information offices** in the old town at ① *Peristil bb, T021-345606*, and on the seafront at ① *Obala Hrvatskog narodnog preporoda 9, T021 360 066, www.visitsplit.com*. The **Turistički Biro** on the seafront at ① *Obala Hrvatskog narodnog preporoda 12, T021-347100, www.turistbiro-split.hr*, deals with private accommodation in and around Split

### Dioklecijanova Palača

The heart of the city lies within the massive walls of Diocletian's Palace, a splendid third-century structure combining the qualities of an imperial villa and a Roman garrison. Rectangular in plan, this monumental edifice measures approximately 215 m by 180 m, with walls 2 m thick and 25 m high. Each of the four outer walls bears a gate: Zlatna Vrata (Golden Gate), Željezna Vrata (Iron Gate), Srebrena Vrata (Silver Gate) and Mjedna Vrata (Bronze Gate). Originally, there were two main streets: the Decumanus, a transversal street running east-west from Srebrena Vrata to Vrata, and the Cardo, a longitudinal street running from the main entrance, Zlatna Vrata. Both streets were colonnaded, and intersected at the central public meeting space, Peristil. On the east side of Peristil lay the mausoleum, and on the west, Jupiter's Temple. Diocletian's imperial apartments were located on the south side of the palace, overlooking the sea, while the servants' and soldiers' quarters overlooked the main land entrance. The stone used to build the palace

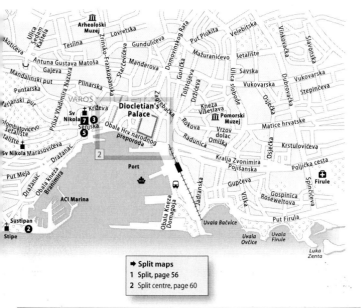

➡ **Split maps**
1  Split, page 56
2  Split centre, page 60

## Robert Adam

The first detailed plans and drawings of how Diocletian's Palace must have once looked were published in 1764, by the Scottish neoclassical architect, Robert Adam, in *The Ruins of the Palace of the Emperor Diocletian at Spalato in Dalmatia*. Adam, who is generally regarded as the greatest British architect of the 18th century, was fascinated by the scale and quality of Diocletian's building projects, and stayed in Split for five weeks in 1757 to investigate the palace. By asking permission to enter people's houses and inspecting their walls, he managed to trace the original Roman structure through the medieval buildings. This was no easy task – the Venetian governor of the time suspected the Scot of spying and nearly had him deported. Fortunately, Adam completed his research, and the space and symmetry of Diocletian's Palace is said to have inspired some of his greatest buildings, which in turn became models for neoclassical architects throughout Europe.

came from the nearby quarries of Brač and Trogir. From the early Middle Ages onwards, new buildings were erected within the palace, so that the original Roman layout has been largely obscured.

### Riva (Seafront promenade)

ⓘ *Obala hrvatskog narodnog preporoda.*

In Roman times, the south façade of the palace rose directly from the sea, and ships would have docked immediately in front of the palace walls. Today it gives onto Obala Hrvatskog narodnog preporoda (better known to locals as the Riva, from the Italian, *riva*, meaning 'shore'), a pedestrian-only promenade, lined with palm trees and open-air cafés. In 2007, the Riva was given a €1.3 million facelift, with the installation of controversial new concrete paving and modern, white, retractable awnings for the café terraces. The project was proposed by 3LHD architects from Zagreb.

### Podrum

ⓘ *Between Obala Hrvatskog narodnog preporoda and Peristil. Daily 0600-2300.*

From the Riva, the Mjedna Vrata (Bronze Gate) leads into the underground chambers, which would originally have used as storerooms and maybe a prison. Today, through daylight hours the main passageway, lined with stalls selling handmade souvenirs, is kept open and leads onto Peristil. Besides the main passageway, the rest of substructures is occasionally accessible (variable hours).

### Peristil

Ever since Roman times, this spacious central courtyard has been the main public meeting place within the palace walls. It is here that Diocletian would have made his public appearances – probably flanked by a guard, and dressed in a silk toga – and his subjects would have kneeled or even prostrated themselves before him.

The two longer sides of the square are lined with marble columns, topped by Corinthian capitals and richly ornamented cornices linked by arches. On the east side, Diocletian's mausoleum (now the cathedral), is guarded by a black granite Egyptian sphinx dating back to 1500 BC. On the west side, the Roman arches have been incorporated into the 15th-century Grisogono-Cipci Palace, now housing Luxor Café.

At the south end of the square, immediately above the podrum exit, four columns mark the monumental arched gateway to the Vestibule, a domed space that served as the main entrance into Diocletian's private living quarters.

## Katedrala Sveti Duje

ⓘ *Peristil, May-Sep daily 0800-2000, Oct-Apr daily 0800-1800, bell tower: daily May-Sep 0900-1900, Oct-Apr variable (depending on the weather), 10Kn.*

Diocletian's mausoleum, an octagonal structure surrounded by 24 columns, now forms the main body of the Cathedral of St Domnius. Before the third century, to prevent the spread of disease, dead bodies (no matter how illustrious) were disposed of outside the city walls. However, Diocletian had raised the Emperor's status to that of divine, so as an 'immortal' he was to be an exception. Upon his death, he was laid to rest here, though his body later mysteriously disappeared.

During the seventh century, refugees from Salona converted the mausoleum into an early Christian church, ironically dedicating it to Sv Duje, after Bishop Domnius of Salona, who Diocletian had had beheaded in AD 304 for sowing the seeds of Christianity.

In 1214, local sculptor Andrije Buvina carved the wooden cathedral doors (now kept behind glass screens in the main entrance). They are quite magnificent, ornamented with reliefs portraying 28 scenes from the life of Christ.

The interior space is round in plan: eight columns with Corinthian capitals support a central dome (symbolizing the Emperor's divine nature), which would originally have been decorated with golden mosaics.

In front of the main entrance, the elegant 60-m Romanesque-Gothic bell tower was constructed in stages between the 12th and 16th centuries, but it then collapsed at the end of the 19th century and had to be rebuilt in 1908. If you have a good head for heights, climb to the top for a bird's-eye view of the palace layout.

## Galerija Vidović

ⓘ *Poljana Kraljice Jelene bb, T021-360155, www.galerija-vidovic.com. Jun-Sep Tue-Fri 0900-2100, Sat-Sun 0900-1600, Mon closed; Oct-May Tue-Fri 0900-1600, Sat-Sun 1000-1300, Mon closed,10Kn.*

Opened in spring 2007, the long-awaited Vidović Gallery displays bold oil paintings of local sights by Split's best-known painter, Emanuel Vidović (1870-1953). He donated these works to the city when he died.

## Pazar

ⓘ *Just outside the eastern wall of Diocletian's Palace. Mon-Sat 0700-1300, Sun 0700-1100.*

Split's open-air fruit and vegetable market is held daily just outside the palace walls. It's well worth a look to size up the season's fresh produce: spinach, wild asparagus and strawberries in spring; tomatoes, peaches and melons in summer; grapes, pomegranates and walnuts in autumn; and cabbages, potatoes and oranges in winter. Dalmatians prefer local seasonal produce – while choice may be limited, quality is assured.

## Zlatna Vrata

The largest and most monumental of the four palace gates, the Golden Gate originally opened onto the road to the nearby Roman settlement of Salona (see page 63). It was walled up during the 14th century, and only uncovered again during the 19th century. Just outside the gate stands a colossal bronze statue of Grgur Ninski (Bishop Gregory of Nin) by Ivan Meštrović. The ninth-century bishop infuriated Rome by campaigning for the use of the Slav language in the Croatian Church, as opposed to Latin. The statue of him was created in 1929 and placed on Peristil (where its proportions must have been daunting) to mark the 1000th anniversary of the Split Synod. Under Italian occupation in 1941, the statue was seen as a symbol of Croatian nationalism and promptly removed. It was re-erected here in 1957. Touch the big toe on the left foot of the bronze statue of Grgur Ninski; it is considered good luck, and has been worn gold by hopeful passers-by.

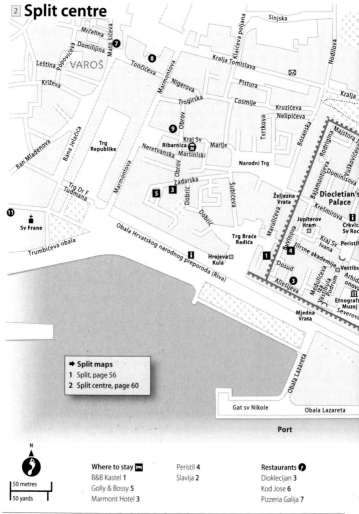

## 2 Split centre

➡ Split maps
1 Split, page 56
2 Split centre, page 60

N

50 metres
50 yards

Where to stay 🛏
B&B Kastel 1
Golly & Bossy 5
Marmont Hotel 3

Peristil 4
Slavija 2

Restaurants 🍴
Dioklecijan 3
Kod Jose 6
Pizzeria Galija 7

## Narodni Trg

Immediately west of Diocletian's Palace lies Split's medieval old town. Here life centres on the Narodni Trg (People's Square), better known to locals as Pjaca, from the Italian, 'piazza'. Paved with gleaming white marble, this is contemporary Split's main square, and you'll find a number of open-air cafés, where you can happily sit and watch the world go by. In the middle of the square stands the former Town Hall, constructed under Venice in 1443, and easily recognized by its three pointed Gothic arches. Nowadays it is used to host temporary art exhibitions.

### Ribarnica

ⓘ *Kraj Sv Marije Mon-Sat 0700-1300, Sun 0700-1100.*

West of Narodni Trg, at the covered fish market you'll find a daily selection of fresh fish and seafood. Locals also call it *peškurija*, from the Italian *pescaria*.

### Varoš

West of the centre, built into the hill leading up to Marjan, Varoš is a labyrinth of winding cobbled streets and traditional Dalmatian stone cottages, dating back to the 17th century. The oldest church in Varoš is the tiny 12th-century Romanesque Sv Nikola (St Nicholas), hidden away in the side street of Stagnja.

### Galerija Umjetina

ⓘ *Kralja Tomislava 15, T021-350112, www.galum.hr. Jun-Sep Mon 1100-1600, Tue-Fri 1100-1900, Sat 1100-1500, Sun closed; Oct-May Mon 0900-1400, Tue-Fri 0900-1700, Sat 0900-1300, Sun closed, 20Kn.*

Behind the palace, near the Golden Gate, the Gallery of Fine Arts reopened in May 2009 following renovation. Centring on an internal courtyard garden, it extends over two floors.

The permanent exhibition features icons, old masters, and modern and contemporary art. Croatian works predominate, notably 19th-century portraits of European aristocrats by Vlaho Bukovac, hazy Dalmatian seascapes by Emanuel Vidović, and bronze sculptures by Ivan Meštrović. There are also several pieces by important European artists, including Paolo Veneziano and Egon Schiele. On the ground floor, **Café Galerija** is open daily 0800-2300.

### Pomorski Muzej

ⓘ *Glagoljaška 18, T021-347346, www.hpms.hr. Mid-Jun to mid-Sep, Mon-Fri 0900-1900, Sat 0900-100, Sun closed; Mid-Sep to mid-Jun Mon-Wed and Fri 0900-1430, Thu 0900-1900, Sat 0900-1300, 10Kn.*

A 10-minute walk east of the palace walls, past the old stone cottages of Radunica, brings you to the 17th-century Gripe Fortress, built by the Venetians. Inside is the Maritime Museum. There are two distinct sections, one dedicated to naval war and the other to naval trading. You'll see scale models of ships, sailing equipment and a fine collection of early 20th-century naval paintings by Alexander Kircher. Of particular note are the world's first torpedoes, made in Rijeka in 1866, designed by a Croat, Ivan Blaž Lupis, and manufactured by an Englishman, Robert Whitehead.

### Marjan

West of the historic centre, a 15-minute uphill hike through Varoš brings you to **Vidilica Café** (see page 79), where an ample terrace offers panoramic views over the city. From here you can begin to explore Marjan, a nature reserve planted with Aleppo pines, holm oak, cypresses and Mediterranean shrubs such as rosemary and broom, located on a compact peninsula, 3.5 km long. From Vidilica, a path along the southside of Marjan leads to the 13th-century Romanesque church of Sv Nikola (St Nicholas) and, further on, to the 15th-century church of Sv Jere (St Jerome), built on the remains of an ancient temple. At the western tip of Marjan, Bene is a recreation area with a family beach, a bar and sports facilities.

### Sustipan

The gardens of Sustipan, planted with elegant cypress trees and dotted with benches, offer views out to sea, and over the ACI Marina back to town. A Benedictine monastery was established here in the 11th century, only to be abandoned 300 years later – some ruins from that time can still be seen. The centrepiece to the gardens is a neoclassical pavilion, erected by the French when Split spent a brief period under Napoleon's Illyrian Provinces.

### Muzej Hrvatskih Arheoloških Spomenika

ⓘ *Šetalište Ivana Meštrovića bb, 2 km west of town, T021-323901, www.mhas-split.hr. Mon-Fri 0900-1600, Sat 0900-1400, 10Kn.*

Overlooking the sea and sheltered to the north by Marjan Hill, you'll find the Museum of Croatian Archaeological Monuments. It displays early Croatian religious art from between the seventh and 12th centuries. Unfortunately only one floor is now in use, many exhibits having been lent to other museums abroad. However, worth seeing are the stone carvings decorated with plaitwork design. In the garden are *stečci*, stone tombs dating back to the cult of the Bogomils, an anti-imperial sect that developed in the Balkans during the 10th century.

### Galerija Meštrović

ⓘ *Šetalište Ivana Meštrovića 46, T021-340800, www.mestrovic.hr. May-Sep Tue-Sun 0900-1900; Oct-Apr Tue-Sat 0900-1600, Sun 0900-1500, 30Kn.*

Close to the Museum of Croatian Archaeological Monuments lies one of Split's most delightful cultural institutions: the Meštrović Gallery. Croatian sculptor Ivan Meštrović designed this monumental villa in the early 1930s, and used it as his summer residence and studio until fleeing the country during the Second World War. On display in the villa and the garden are 200 sculptures and reliefs, in wood, marble, stone and bronze, created between the beginning of the century and 1946. The entrance ticket is also valid for the Holy Cross Chapel within Kaštelet, a 17th-century complex bought by Meštrović in 1932, which is situated 100 m down the road at Šetalište Ivana Meštrovića 39. Here you can see a cycle of New Testament wood carvings, that are considered to be Meštrović's finest work.

## Beaches

Locals generally prefer to go to the islands. However, the main city beach at **Bačvica** (a 10-minute walk southeast of the old town) is clean and functional; it is possible to rent a sunlounger and umbrella, and there are showers and bars. **Bene** (4 km west of the old town), on the tip of Marjan Peninsula, offers a number of small, secluded, rocky coves backed by pine trees; there are also showers and a bar.

---

# Around Split → *For listings, see pages 74-85.*

## Salona

Just outside the modern town of Solin, 6 km north of Split, Salona is Croatia's most important archaeological site. As the largest Roman settlement on the Dalmatian coast, during the third century it is said to have had a population approaching 60,000, who were catered for by a forum, temples, an amphitheatre and therme (baths).

Following the legalization of Christianity in AD 313, a Christian community rapidly developed here, and in the early fifth century Salona's bishop became the Metropolitan of the province of Dalmatia. Many churches were built on the Salona site, and the centre moved from the Forum to what is now Manastirine, where a basilica was built over the site of Domnius' grave.

Salona was devastated by the Avars and Slavs in the seventh century, and has lain in ruins ever since. It was the surviving Salonites who founded Split, when they fled to Diocletian's Palace for shelter following the destruction of their homes.

**Arheološki Kompleks Salone** ⓘ *Put Starina bb, Solin, T021-212900. May-Oct Mon-Fri 0700-1900, Sat 0900-1900, Sun 0900-1300, Nov-Apr Mon-Fri 0900-1530, Sat 0900-1400, Sun closed, 20Kn.* At first glance, the Salona Archaeological Site is an overgrown landscape of crumbling stones and fallen columns, but with a site plan (available at the entrance) and a little imagination, you can begin to visualize how it looked as a prosperous Roman settlement.

Manastirine, immediately south of the entrance, is the place where the early Christians buried their martyrs, notably Bishop Domnius. It subsequently became a place of worship, and countless sarcophagi were placed around the bishop's tomb. In the early fifth century a triple-nave basilica was built over the site. The foundations, sections of the crumbling walls and several sarcophagi can still be seen today. Nearby, you can see the second-century *therme* (Roman baths), which opened onto a central courtyard with a large pool.

Built into a hillside in the northwest corner of the site stands Salona's most impressive building, an amphitheatre from the late second century. It was designed to seat 18,000 spectators, and gladiators and wild animals, and later Christians, would have fought here. In the sixth century, Byzantine Emperor Justinian banned gladiator fights, and it was probably used instead for religious and defensive purposes.

If you're based in Split, Trogir, a short distance up the coast, with its magnificent UNESCO-listed medieval cathedral, makes a perfect half-day trip out of town. Following the coast further north, you arrive at Šibenik, home to another splendid cathedral, this time Gothic-Renaissance, and an old town built into a hillside overlooking the sea. Inland from Šibenik, Krka National Park comprises a wooded gorge with a series of spectacular thundering waterfalls.

## Trogir

Tiny Trogir, 27 km west of Split, sits compact on a small island, connected to the mainland by one bridge and tied to the outlying island of Čiovo by a second. **Trogir** tourist office at ① *Trg Ivana Pavla II 1, T021-885628, www.tztrogir.hr.*

Founded by Greeks from Issa (on the island of Vis) in the third century BC, today Trogir is a romantic huddle of narrow cobbled streets and medieval stone buildings. Once protected by 15th-century city walls, a labyrinth of narrow cobbled streets twists its way between the medieval houses bringing you out on to a splendid main square, overlooked by a monumental 13th-century Romanesque cathedral. In 1997, Trogir was listed a UNESCO World Heritage Site and it is well worth a visit.

The south-facing seafront promenade is lined with cafés and restaurants, and there are also a couple of good, reasonably priced hotels. Just across the narrow Trogir Channel, on the island of Čiovo, a well-equipped marina makes a base for several companies chartering yachts.

**Katedrala Sveti Lovrijenac** ① *Trg Ivana Pavla II, T021-881550, Jun-Sep Mon-Sat 0800-1800, Sun 1200-1800; May and Oct 0800-1200 and 1600-1800; Nov-Apr on request, 25Kn (entry to cathedral and bell-tower).* On Trogir's main square, the Romanesque Cathedral of St Lawrence is a splendid example of medieval architecture. Constructed between 1213 and 1250, its most impressive feature is the main portal, which is sheltered within a spacious vestibule edged by a marble banquette, and adorned with elaborately detailed Romanesque sculpture by Master Radovan. The great door is flanked by a pair of burly lions that form pedestals for the figures of Adam and Eve. Around the portal, scenes from the Bible are mixed with references to everyday peasant life, in an extraordinary orgy of saints, apostles, animals and grotesques.

Inside, the cathedral is dimly lit. Look out for the 15th-century chapel to the left of the main aisle, featuring St John of Trogir lying upon a stone sarcophagus, watched over by statues of Mary, Christ, the saints and the apostles.

The cathedral also boasts an elegant 47-m bell tower. Building began in the early 15th century, and took place in successive stages – the first two storeys are Gothic, while the third and final level, in Renaissance style, was completed in 1610. You can climb to the top for stunning views across the ancient rooftops.

## Šibenik

**Arriving in Šibenik** **Šibenik bus station** ① *Draga 14, T060-368368,* lies on the seafront and is a five-minute walk from the city centre. **Šibenik train station** ① *Milete bb, T022-333699,* south of the bus station, a 10-minute walk from the city centre. **Šibenik tourist office** ① *Obala Dr F Tudjmana 5, T022-214411, www.sibenik-tourism.hr,* has a walk-in information centre on the seafront. **Šibenik and Knin County Tourist Board** ① *Fra Nikole Ruži a bb, Šibenik, T022-219072, www.sibenikregion.com.*

**Places in Šibenik** Some 75 km northwest of Split, Šibenik lies in a protected sea channel, at the mouth of the River Krka. The medieval old town is a warren of steep, winding alleyways and terracotta-roofed houses, built into a hillside below the remains of a Venetian fortress. Close to the seafront, the city's main sight is the monumental Renaissance Cathedral of St Jacob, which is included on the UNESCO list of World Heritage Sites.

On the edge of town, disused factories and sprawling modern suburbs reveal a period of 20th-century industrial development followed by economic collapse caused by the war. However, Šibenik comes to life each year in August, when it stages the four-day Terraneo alternative music festival (see Festivals, page 83).

**Katedrala Sv Jakova** ① *Trg Republike Hrvatske. May-Sep daily 0830-2000, Oct-Apr 0830-1200 and 1600-2000, 15Kn*. Built between 1431 and 1536, the splendid Cathedral of St Jacob was constructed in several stages. The result, a mix of late Gothic and Renaissance styles, is a three-aisle basilica based on the plan of a Latin cross, with a trefoil façade and cupola. The project was initiated by Venetian architects, who worked here for 10 years. They were responsible for the ornate Gothic portals – the main door portrays The Last Judgement, surrounded by the Apostles and crowned by a portrait of Christ, and the side door, the Entrance to Paradise, guarded on either side by a lion, one carrying Adam and the other Eve. In 1441, Juraj Dalmatinac, a Dalmatian from Zadar, who had trained as an architect in Venice, took over. He proposed a far grander edifice, a three-aisle basilica topped by an octagonal cupola, introducing the newly emerging Renaissance style. He also created one of the building's best-loved features – a frieze running around the outer walls, made up of 74 faces, some moustachioed, some turbanned, said to be those citizens too stingy to contribute to the cost of the building. Sadly, Dalmatinac died in 1473, before his masterpiece was completed. The final works were conducted by one of his pupils, Nikola Fiorentinac, who oversaw the mounting of the cupola and the construction of the vaulted roof, employing a unique system of interlocking monolithic stone slabs cut to shape.

The baptistery was designed by Dalmatinac but completed by another of his pupils, Andrija Aleši, an Albanian from Durres. It is to the right of the main altar, and is accessed by a short flight of stone steps. It is an enchanting space, with decorative stonework. The final stone of the building was laid in 1536, and in 1555 it was dedicated to St Jacob.

**Krka National Park** ① *16 km north of Šibenik. The National Park office is in Šibenik at Trg Ivana Pavla II 5, T021-201777, www.npkrka.hr. Jun-Sep daily 0800-1900, 95Kn, Mar-May and Oct daily 0900-1700, 80Kn, Nov-Feb daily 0900-1500, 30Kn. National park boats leave from Skradin for Skradinski Buk on the hour, departing for the return journey on the half hour. The cost of the ride is included in the entrance ticket.*
Krka National Park encompasses a steep-sided, wooded canyon and a series of seven waterfalls. The main entrance is close to Skradinski Buk, the park's most spectacular falls, made up of a series of 17 cascades plunging over 40 m into a wide emerald-green basin, ideal for bathing. Next to the falls, a meadow, bordered by woods, offers an idyllic spot for picnicking. Above Skradinski Buk, a series of wooden bridges and well-marked footpaths lead to the next falls, Roški slap, 10 km to the north. If you don't fancy the hike, it's possible to catch a second national park boat, which runs several times a day, shuttling visitors between the two falls and calling en route at the 15th-century Visovac Samostan (Visovac Monastery) perched on a small island in the middle of Visovačko Jezero (Visovac Lake).

## Southeast of Split → *For listings, see pages 74-85.*

South of Split the coastal highway (Magistrala) twists and turns to follow the water's edge, affording fine views over the sea and islands to your right, and the rugged silhouette of the Dinaric Mountains to your left. A succession of coastal villages offers modest pebble beaches and rooms to rent in 1970s concrete-block houses mellowed by draping vines and balconies lined with potted geraniums. The most interesting destinations are Omiš, at the mouth of the Cetina Valley, and Makarska, at the foot of Biokovo mountain, on the so-called Makarska Rivijera.

### Omiš

Some 28 km southeast of Split, Omiš lies where the River Cetina emerges from a dramatic gorge to meet the sea. Many people pass straight through, but closer inspection reveals old stone houses and cobbled alleys, a colourful roadside fruit and vegetable market and a small harbour. The scene is presided over by a hilltop fortress backed by the spectacular Omiška Dinara Mountains.

Centuries ago, the people of Omiš were fearsome medieval pirates, who would raid Byzantine and Venetian ships, then sail away up the gorge, out of sight. Today, the town makes an ideal base for exploring the Cetina Gorge, where various agencies organize adventure sports.

There's a town beach just south of the centre, though it's somewhat spoilt by the nearby traffic. Better still, head for Mimice (12 km southeast), where you'll find a lovely curving pebble beach backed by baked by a hillside village.

**Omiš tourist office** is at ① *Trg Kneza Miroslava bb, T021-861350, www.tz-omis.hr.*

### Rijeka Cetina

With its source in the Dinara Mountains, the River Cetina runs through a gentle valley of green meadows, which in turn becomes a dramatic landscape of spectacular karst formations, the Cetina Gorge. Cutting a high-sided canyon between the mountains of Mosor and Biokovo, it then meets the sea at Omiš. A series of rapids makes the river ideal for rafting, canoeing and kayaking, while the sheer-faced cliffs attract free-climbing enthusiasts (see What to do, page 84). Riverside restaurants serve up freshwater specialities such as trout, eels and frogs, making a welcome change from the omnipresent seafood of the coast.

### Makarska

Through summer Makarska makes a perfect base for exploring the so-called Makarska Rivijera, a 60-km stretch of coast offering some of the best mainland beaches, while keen walkers are drawn to the rugged landscapes and rural villages of Biokovo Nature Park during spring and autumn.

**Arriving in Makarska** **Makarska bus station** ① *T021-612333*, is on the main road above town. **Jadrolinija** ① *www.jadrolinija.hr*, runs daily ferries from Makarska to Sumartin on the eastern tip of the island of Brač. **Makarska tourist office** is at ① *Obala Kralja Tomislava 16, T021-612002, www.makarska-info.hr.*

**Places in Makarska** Makarska combines the qualities of an old-fashioned Dalmatian port and a modern-day tourist resort. The setting, 67 km southeast of Split, is impressive: a palm-lined seafront promenade, built around a large cove, protected from the open sea by a wooded peninsula to the southwest, and sheltered from the cold bura wind by the craggy limestone heights of Mount Biokovo to the northeast. There's also a pleasant main square, **Kačićeva Trg**, rimmed with 18th-century baroque buildings.

Tourism here dates back to 1914, when the first hotel opened. In the 1970s, a string of modern hotels and houses with rooms to let were built along the coast. Today, come summer it's overrun with young visitors and families from all over Europe, who are drawn by its beaches, vibrant nightlife and reasonably priced accommodation.

**Beaches**  Makarska's town beach, **Donja Luka**, is a 10-minute walk west of the centre and has umbrellas and sun loungers for hire, water sports facilities and beach bars. From here, the coastal path runs 10 km northwest, all the way to Brela, with a string of pebble beaches along the route, several nudist-friendly. East of the centre, a lovely 2-km footpath leads through pinewoods, following the coast, to arrive at **Nugal**, a pebble beach in a small cove backed by steep cliffs, which is popular with nudists.

You might also check out some of the small low-key resorts of the **Makarska Rivijera**, which stretches from Brela in the north to Gradac in the south. Of these, Brela, Baška Voda and Tučepi all have fine pebble beaches and are served by local buses running along the coast from Makarska.

## Mount Biokovo

Behind Makarska, a network of clearly marked footpaths lead up Mount Biokovo, a barren rocky karst landscape with scanty pastures and bare limestone rocks supporting only the hardiest indigenous species, such as chamois goats and mouflon sheep. From Makar, a semi-abandoned cluster of old stone cottages, a well-marked trail leads to the peak of **Vošac** (1440 m), which can be walked in four hours, while another trail departs from Kotišina to reach the same peak in five hours. From Vošac, the terrain becomes increasingly rocky, though hardened hikers can attempt a final 1½-hour pull to the highest peak, **Sveti Jure** (1760 m). The summit is capped by a slightly disheartening radio and TV transmitter, while its namesake, the tiny stone chapel of Sv Jure, is close by, but remains closed for most of the year. On a clear day you can see across the Adriatic Sea to Italy and inland to Bosnia Herzegovina. See What to do, page 84, for agencies organizing hiking tours.

If the hike up looks too stiff, hire a jeep and drive from Makarska up to Sveti Jure (31 km). Take the road for Vrgorac, then swing sharp left for the park and follow a series of hairpin bends to the summit.

As the closest island to Split and the only island in Dalmatia with an airport, Brač has the advantage of being easily accessible. The disadvantage of this, however, is that it has lost a degree of its island identity.

Its largest town and chief ferry port is Supetar. While the bulk of foreigners pass straight through, on their way to the more prestigious resort of Bol, many families from the mainland have summer homes in Supetar itself. It's a pleasant enough place, with the old town focusing on a crescent-shaped harbour, and a decent bathing area, backed by several large hotels, west of the centre. There is little of cultural interest here, though the town cemetery is noted for its beautifully carved tombstones.

The island's top destination is Bol, home to the lovely beach of Zlatni Rat, presided over by Vidova Gora, the highest peak on any of the Adriatic islands. Bol is crawling with tourists during July and August, but if you manage to visit outside peak season it's well worth it for the fantastic beach.

### Arriving on the island of Brač

**Getting there** The main ferry port is Supetar, served by regular daily **Jadrolinija** ① *www. jadrolinija.hr*, ferries from Split. In addition, Jadrolinija also runs a high-speed catamaran from Split to Jelsa (island of Hvar), calling at Bol en route.

**Tourist information Supetar tourist office** ① *Porat 1, T021-630551, www.supetar.hr*; **Bol tourist office** ① *Porat bolskih pomoraca bb, T021-635638, www.bol.hr.*

### Bol

On the south coast of Brač, Bol is home to Croatia's most-photographed beach, the spectacular Zlatni Rat. This once-idyllic little fishing village has somewhat lost its charm due to the rampant success brought upon it by its beach – it's one of Croatia's top package destinations, with several big hotels and a miniature train running from the village to the beach – but if you can visit outside peak season, it's more than worth the trip. The village itself is made of old stone cottages clustered round a pretty harbour filled with coloured wooden fishing boats. A short walk east of the harbour, the 15th-century Dominican Monastery is set in gardens overlooking the sea.

### Zlatni Rat

A pleasant tree-lined promenade leads 2 km from the village of Bol to the renowned beach of Zlatni Rat (Golden Cape). The promenade, overlooked by the big package hotels (discreetly hidden by the trees), makes a pleasurable walk (there are no buses). An extraordinary geographical feature, it's composed of fine shingle and runs 500 m perpendicular to the coast, moving and changing its shape slightly from season to season, depending on local winds and currents. It's a perfect beach for children as the water is shallow and the seabed easy on their feet. It's also Croatia's number one site for windsurfing (see What to do, page 84). A cluster of pines at the top end of the cape offer respite from the sun, and there are several bars and kiosks selling cold drinks and snacks. As well as Zlatni Rat there's a stretch reserved for nudists, known as **Paklina**, just 200 m west of the cape.

## Vidova Gora

The highest peak (778 m) on all the Croatian islands, offers a bird's-eye view of Zlatna Rat and Bol, plus distant views of Hvar, Vis, Pelješac Peninsula and Korčula. It's possible to walk or bike up, though the less athletic might opt for a tour by minibus. Enquire at Bol tourist office for details.

## Pustinja Blaca

ⓘ *Closed for restoration at the time of writing, following a fire in 2011.*

The impressive monastery complex of Blaca Hermitage, 13 km west of Bol, is built into the cliffside high above the coast. It's possible to reach Blaca Bay by boat from the harbour in Bol – just as the monks used to do – and then walk up. The hermitage was founded by monks from Poljica, on the mainland, who fled here to escape the Turks in 1550. Originally they took shelter in a cave, subsequently building the church and hermitage, and later opening a printing press and a school for children from nearby hamlets. The last monk to live here, Father Niko Miličević Mladi, was a keen astrologer. He set up an observatory in 1926 and, besides his astronomical tools, left behind a collection of old clocks. Visitors can see these, along with the old-fashioned kitchen, an armoury and a display of period furniture. Blaca is on the UNESCO World Heritage 'Tentative List'.

---

## Island of Hvar → *For listings, see pages 74-85.*

A long, thin island, trendy Hvar is a land of vineyards, lavender fields and old Venetian coastal villages with an altogether slower, more pleasurable way of life than the mainland. The most popular and by far and away the most charming resort is Hvar Town. Close by, on the western end of the island, is Stari Grad, the main ferry port, and Jelsa, a pleasant fishing village and low-key seaside resort. The eastern end of Hvar is sparsely populated and offers little of cultural interest.

## Arriving on the island of Hvar

**Getting there**   The main ferry port is Stari Grad, served by regular Jadrolinija ferries from Split. **Jadrolinija** ⓘ *www.jadrolinija.hr*, also runs a daily catamaran from Split to the island of Lastovo (South Dalmatia), stopping at Hvar Town and Vela Luka (island of Korčula) en route. In addition, the same company runs a high-speed catamaran from Split to Jelsa, calling at Bol (island of Brač) en route.

**Tourist information**   **Hvar Town tourist office** is at ⓘ *Trg Sv Stjepana bb, T021-741059, www.tzhvar.hr*. **Stari Grad tourist office** is at ⓘ *Obala Dr Franje Tuđmana 1, T021-765763, www.stari-grad-faros.hr*. **Jelsa tourist office** is at ⓘ *Riva bb, T021-761017, www.tzjelsa.hr*.

## Hvar Town

Hvar Town is probably Croatia's most fashionable resort after Dubrovnik. Old stone houses are built into the slopes of three hills surrounding a bay, with the highest peak crowned by a Venetian fortress, which is floodlit by night. Café life centres on the magnificent main square, giving directly onto the harbour and backed by a 16th-century cathedral. The bay is protected from the open sea to the south by the scattered Pakleni Otoci (Pakleni islets), which are covered with dense pine forests and rimmed by rocky shores, offering secluded coves for bathing.

Hvar Town is a favourite overnight port of call for sailing boats and many people come here exclusively for the nightlife – it's been billed the Croatian Ibiza. Expect hip design hotels, upmarket seafood eateries, chi-chi cocktail bars and occasional celebrities – recent illustrious visitors include Prince Harry, Beyonce, Tom Cruise, and Roman Abramovich.

**Trg Sv Stjepan** St Stephen's Square, the largest piazza in Dalmatia, dates back to the 13th century. The east end is backed by the cathedral, while the west end opens out onto the Mandrac, an enclosed harbour for small boats, which in turn gives onto the bay. The paving dates from 1780 and in the centre stands a well from 1520. Today many of the old buildings lining the square house popular cafés, restaurants and galleries at street level.

**Katedrala Sv Stjepan** ① *Trg Sv Stjepana bb, Hvar Town, T021-741152. Daily 0900-1300 and 1700-1900, 10Kn.* Providing a majestic backdrop to the main square, St Stephen's Cathedral was built in stages between the 16th and 17th centuries on the foundations of an earlier monastery, to produce a trefoil façade standing in perfect harmony with a four-storey bell tower. There is also a treasury.

**Arsenal i Kazalište** ① *Trg Sv Stjepana bb, Hvar Town.* On the south corner of the main square, looking onto the harbour, the 16th-century Arsenal is easily identified by its huge front arch, which allowed Venetian galleys to dock inside for repair work.

The upper floor houses the theatre, which opened in 1612 and welcomed all citizens regardless of their social standing, making it one of the first institutions of its kind in Europe. Unfortunately it is currently closed for restoration.

**Franjevački Samostan** ① *Križa bb, Hvar Town, T021-741193. May-Oct daily 0900-1300, 1700-1900, Nov-Apr by appointment, 25Kn.* South of the centre, a pleasant seafront path leads to the 15th-century Franciscan Monastery. The entrance is through a charming cloister – used for classical music concerts during the summer festival – into the former refectory, now a museum. The most impressive piece on show is undoubtedly The Last Supper, a vast 17th-century canvas by an unknown Venetian artist, measuring 2.5 m by 8 m.

# Hvar Town

**Where to stay** 🛏
Aparthotel Pharia 3
Green Lizard Hostal 1
Podstine 4
Riva 5

**Restaurants** 🍴
Alviž 6
Konobo Menego 7
Macondo 3

The refectory opens onto a beautiful garden, with a magnificent 300-year-old cypress tree, overlooking the sea.

**Fortica** ① *Hvar Town, Jun-Sep daily 0800-2200, Oct-May by appointment, 25Kn*. Above town, a winding footpath leads through a garden of dense Mediterranean planting, to arrive at the fortress. A medieval castle once stood here, though the present structure was erected by the Venetians in 1557, and the ochre-coloured barracks were added by the Austrian military authorities during the 19th century. From the ramparts, you have fantastic views down onto the town and harbour, and out across the sea to the Pakleni islets.

**Beaches** The nearest beach to the centre of Hvar Town is **Bonj Les Bains**, a concrete bathing area rimmed by a 1930s stone colonnade and overlooked by the vast Hotel Amfora. It's a 10-minute walk west of town, though you need to pay for the sunloungers and private cabanas (reservations recommended, T021-750300).

For a more back-to-nature experience, either hire a sea kayak (see page 84) or take a taxi-boat (0800-2000) from Hvar Town's harbour to the **Pakleni islets**. Covered with dense pine forests and surrounded by rocky shores, they offer secluded pebble coves for bathing. The nearest islet, **Jerolim**, is predominantly nudist, while the largest, **Sveti Klement**, is home to an ACI sailing marina and the lovely boho-chic retreat of Palmižana (see Where to stay, page 76).

To join the see-and-be seen crowd, head for **Stipanksa** (also one of the Pakleni islets), where **Carpe Diem Stipanska** ① *www.carpe-diem-beach.com, Jun-Sep 1000-1900*, is a smart beach club with a pool, restaurant, bar, two beach areas lined with palm umbrellas and teak lounge chairs, a beach volleyball court and a diving centre. They also arrange Full Moon parties and other late-night events through July and August – Boy George has been guest DJ here on several occasions.

## Around Hvar

**Stari Grad** Stari Grad is Hvar's oldest settlement and chief ferry port. It's a more relaxed, slightly less swish resort than Hvar Town, with an easygoing village atmosphere. Founded by Greeks from the Aegean island of Paros in 385 BC, it was originally known as Pharos. Little of the original Greek settlement remains today, other than the 11-m-long **Cyclop's Wall**, now a UNESCO World Heritage Site, which is made up of massive stone blocks and can be traced through some of the buildings on the south side of the bay.

Today, most of the buildings in the old part of town date from the 16th and 17th centuries – the best examples can be seen on Škor, a picturesque square enclosed by baroque houses. There aren't many great beaches or decent hotels, and little of cultural interest other than the 16th-century Hektorović House, but you will find several excellent seafood restaurants here, which much more reasonably priced than those in Hvar Town.

**Tvrdalj** ① *Trg Tvrdalj, Stari Grad, T021-765068; Jul-Sep daily 1000-1300, 1800-2000, May-Jun and Oct daily 1000-1300, Nov-Apr closed, 10Kn*, Stari Grad's best-loved building is the fortified Hektorović House, on the south side of the bay, in the old town. It was built by Petar Hektorović (1487-1572) in 1520, as a home for him and his friends, and also as a place of refuge for the entire town, in the event of a Turkish invasion. Hektorović was a local aristocratic landowner, who had been educated in Italy and became one of Dalmatia's most prominent Renaissance poets. Tvrdalj's centrepiece is a long rectangular fishpond, surrounded by a fine cloister, around which the living quarters, domestic area and servant quarters are arranged. The walls of the interior bear many plaques, with witty and philosophical inscriptions in both Croatian and Latin, and there's a walled garden where Hektorović cultivated both indigenous Mediterranean and exotic plants.

**Jelsa** Jelsa is a lively fishing town and seaside resort, built around a natural harbour, 10 km east of Stari Grad. Everyday life focuses on the 19th-century seafront promenade, lined with cheerful cafés and pizzerias, while to each side of the bay, dense pinewoods have been used to conceal a number of large hotel complexes, built during the 1970s.

Jelsa in connected to Bol on the island of Brač by a daily catamaran service – something to bear in mind if you want to visit both islands without returning to Split first.

**Humac** A poorly maintained local road leads 8 km east of Jelsa all the way to Sučuraj, on the eastern tip of the island. If you follow this road for 8 km, you'll see a sign to the right for Humac. Walk the final 400 m along a rough track, to arrive at a romantic cluster of abandoned stone cottages, founded as a temporary dwelling for shepherds in the 16th century. No one lives here anymore, but during summer it's possible to eat at the unforgettable **Konoba Humac** (see Restaurants, page 81).

A 30-minute walk from Humac, **Grapčeva Špilja** is a vast chamber of underground stalactites and stalagmites, with traces of human civilization from the third millennium BC. Through summer (June to September) you can visit the cave with a guide. Contact Jelsa tourist office for details.

---

## Island of Vis → *For listings, see pages 74-85.*

Closed to foreigners until 1989 due to the presence of a Yugoslav naval base, Croatia's most distant inhabited island was spared the commercial brand of tourism that flourished along much of the Adriatic during the 1970s. It's now rapidly developing into a discreet but rather upmarket destination, thanks to its wild, rugged landscapes and the insight it offers into the way people once lived throughout Dalmatia. The two main settlements, Vis Town and Komiža, both lie on the coast, while there are also about a dozen semi-abandoned inland villages. There is limited holiday accommodation, but the restaurants are truly wonderful, the wines, notably the white Vugava and the red Viški Plavac, are organically produced, and there are several peaceful beaches where you can soak up the sun and swim in crystal-clear waters, said to be among the cleanest in the Adriatic.

### Arriving on the island of Vis
**Getting there** The main ferry port is in Vis Town, served by daily **Jadrolinija** ① *www. jadrolinija.hr*, ferries from Split.

**Tourist information** Vis Town tourist office is at ① *Šetalište Stare Isse 5, T021-717017, www. tz-vis.hr.* **Komiža tourist office** is at ① *Riva Sv Mikule 2, T021-713455, www.tz-komiza.hr.*

### Vis Town
On the north coast of Vis, this is the island's largest town and chief port. The ancient Greeks founded Issa, their first colony in Dalmatia, on the slopes above the northwest part of the bay, in 389 BC. Unfortunately there's not much left of it today, but excavations have unearthed finds now on display in the archaeological museums in both Split and Vis itself. The Vis Town you see today grew out of two separate settlements, Kut and Luka, which

have joined together to form a 3-km string of buildings, ranging from humble fishermen's cottages to noble baroque villas, hugging the large sheltered bay. Jutting out into the bay, Prirov Peninsula is capped by a proud 16th-century Franciscan monastery. The entire scene is backed by craggy hills, promising the wild, unspoilt landscapes of the interior. Through summer, yachts moor up along the seafront, their crews drawn by Vis's authentic fish restaurants and fine wines.

## Komiža

On the west coast of Vis, 18 km southwest of Vis Town, this friendly fishing village is built around a small harbour. Old stone buildings with wooden shutters and terracotta-tiled roofs line a series of narrow alleys, each of which runs down to the seafront. Here, locals of all generations meet for morning coffee, conduct their evening promenade and put the world to rights. Above the village, from the weather-beaten slopes of Hum Hill, a 13th-century monastery surveys the open waters of the Adriatic and the outlying islet of Biševo, home to the Blue Cave. Through winter 20 or so fishing boats animate the harbour but, come summer, elegant yachts from all parts of Europe call here. It's probably one of the most unspoilt places on all the islands in a fantastic setting and with excellent restaurants.

## Modra Spilja

On the east coast of the islet of Biševo, 5 km southwest of Komiža, Biševo's Blue Cave is often compared to the Blue Cave on Capri, Italy. Some 24 m long, 12 m wide and with water 10-20 m deep, sunlight enters the cave through a submerged side entrance, passes through the water and reflects off the seabed, casting the interior in a magnificent shade of blue. Small boats ferry visitors in and out to see this natural wonder. You can visit the cave as part of an organized day trip from Komiža. Excursions are planned so you enter the cave around midday when the light is at its best, then continue to the west side of Biševo for a few hours in Porat Uvala (Porat Bay), where there's a pleasant sand beach and a couple of simple restaurants. Boats depart at 0900 (weather permitting) from the harbour and return at 1700. Enquire at Komiža tourist office for further details.

## Beaches

In Komiža, the main town beach, **Gospa Guzarica**, lies west of the centre in front of Hotel Komiža and has a diving club. Southeast of Komiža town centre, **Kamenica** beach is home to the **Aquarius** ① www.aquariuskomiza.com, open-air club. Some of the best beaches are on the southeast coast of Vis. If you have a car, head for Rukavac, where you'll find **Uvala Srebrena** (Silver Bay), a popular bathing spot backed by pinewoods with a series of white rocky ledges stepping down to the water, or Milna, where the small beach in **Uvala Zaglav** (Zaglav Bay) offers shallow water suitable for kids.

## Central Dalmatian Coast listings

*For hotel and restaurant price codes and other relevant information, see pages 12-19.*

### 🛏 Where to stay

**Split** *p56, maps p56 and p60*
#### Diocletian's Palace and the historic centre
**€€€ Hotel Marmont**, Zadarska 13, T021-308060, www.marmonthotel.com. Opened in summer 2008, this chic hotel occupies a restored 15th-century building near Narodni Trg, the main square. It has 21 smart rooms with minimalist furniture and oak floors, flat-screen TV and Wi-Fi. There's also a 1st-floor terrace café with potted olive trees.

**€€ Hotel B&B Kaštel 1700**, Mihovilova Sirina 5, T021-343912, www.kastelsplit.com. Brilliantly located, overlooking the palm-lined seafront promenade, but entered from around the back, off Vočni Trg. There are 10 rooms, all with wooden floors and simple furniture, plus a/c, satellite TV, minibar and hairdryer. The staff are friendly and helpful, there's an internet corner next to reception, plus a breakfast room with exposed Roman stone walls.

**€€ Hotel Peristil**, Poljana Kraljice Jelena 5, T021-329070, www.hotelperistil.com. Within the palace walls, next to Srebrena Vrata, this small hotel has 12 rooms – the best ones have views onto the Roman Peristil and the cathedral. Restaurant, great location, helpful staff, plus a lovely terrace out front where breakfast is served in summer.

**€€ Hotel Slavija**, Buvinova 2, T021-323840, www.hotelslavija.com. Within the walls of Diocletian's Palace, this building dates from the 17th century and has been a hotel since 1900, making it the oldest in town. It was fully renovated in 2004 and now has 25 basic but comfortable rooms. The location is fantastic, if you don't mind the noise from surrounding bars. The best rooms are on the top floor and have private terraces.

**€€ Salvezani Apartments**, Dominisova 10, T021-344392, www.splitapartment.info. In a beautifully restored 17th-century stone building, within the palace walls, close to Zlatna Vrata, these 3 self-catering apartments each sleep 2. They're tastefully furnished, and have wooden floors, wooden beamed ceilings, and some exposed medieval stonework.

**€ Golly & Bossy**, Morpurgova Poljana 2, T021-510999, www.gollybossy.com. This slick modern hostel occupies a former department store, with the escalator still in use. There are 28 rooms, ranging from doubles to 8-bed dorms, and a ground floor bar-restaurant with tables out front below big white umbrellas. The name comes from 'goli i bosi', which means 'naked and barefoot' in Croatian.

#### Outside the historic centre
**€€ Villa Matejuška**, Tomića stine 3, T098-222822, www.villamatejuska.hr. In a narrow cobbled alley in Varoš, 1 block back from the seafront, this old stone building has been renovated to make a small family-run hotel. There are 6 apartments, each with a (small) shower, a/c, satellite TV, Wi-Fi and a fully equipped kitchenette. The same family run the ground-floor **Konoba Matejuška** (see page 78).

**€ Villa Varoš**, Miljenko Smoje 1, T021-483469, www.villavaros.hr. In Varoš, this small family-run hotel occupies a traditional Dalmatian stone building with green wooden window shutters. There are 8 basic but comfortable rooms, plus 1 apartment with a terrace and jacuzzi. Breakfast (not included in price, but hotel guests get a discount) is served at the nearby Konoba Leut, looking out over the fishing boats of Matejuška.

**Trogir** *p64*
**€€ Hotel Pašike**, Sinjska bb, T021-885185, www.hotelpasike.com. This small hotel in

the old town has 14 rooms with antique furniture and modern en suite bathrooms, plus one apartment with a hydro-massage tub. On the ground floor, Konoba Pašike serves barbecued Dalmatian meat and fish dishes at outdoor tables, with live music.

**€€ Hotel Tragos**, Budislavićeva 3, T021-884729, www.tragos.hr. In an 18th-century baroque palace in the old town, Tragos has 12 simply furnished, modern rooms, decorated in warm creams and yellows. In the courtyard garden, Restaurant Tragos serves Dalmatian favourites such as *pasticada* (beef stewed in sweet wine) and *brudet* (fish stewed in a tomato and onion). They also offer free parking and transfers to and from the airport.

### Šibenik and around *p64*
**€ Agrotourism Kalpić**, Kalpići 4, Lozovac, T091-5845520, www.kalpic.com. 15 km from Šibenik, on the road to Drniš and close to Krka National Park, this welcoming farm offers eight double rooms, furnished with antiques. They do a generous cooked-to-order breakfast (optional) plus dinner on request, with everything prepared from their own farm produce.

**€ Hostel Indigo**, Jurja Barakovića 3, T022-200159 www.hostel-indigo.com. In Šibenik's old town, this small hostel offers 4-bed rooms with lockers and free Wi-Fi, plus a common room with TV, and optional breakfast.

**€ Hotel Skradinski Buk**, Burinovac bb, Skradin, T022-771771, www.skradinskibuk. hr. On the edge of Krka National Park, this small family-run hotel occupies a carefully renovated old stone building in the centre of Skradin. There are 25 rooms and 4 suites, and a ground floor restaurant with a terrace.

### Omiš *p66*
**€€ Hotel Villa Dvor**, Mosorska cesta 13, T021-863444, www.hotel-villadvor.hr. Built into a cliff overlooking the River Cetina, this hotel has 23 comfortable rooms and a terrace restaurant affording impressive views onto the canyon. It's approached up a steep flight of 106 stone steps – a lift was installed in 2012 to make it more accessible. The hotel boat shuttles guests down the river to nearby beaches.

### Makarska *p66*
**€€ Hotel Biokovo**, Obala Kralja Tomislava bb, T021-615244, www.hotelbiokovo.hr. Comprising 55 rooms and one apartment, this pleasant, old-fashioned hotel in the centre of town was refurbished in 2004, and has a ground floor café and restaurant giving onto the seaside promenade, and a small wellness centre.

**€€ Hotel Maritimo**, Put Cvitačke bb, T021-619900, www.hotel-maritimo.hr. On the coastal path, immediately opposite a pebble beach, a 15-min walk from the Makarska's old town, this modern hotel has 19 rooms and one suite, and a ground floor bar-restaurant with a terrace. It's worth paying a little extra for a sea-view and balcony.

**€€ Hotel Osejava**, Šetalište Dr Fra Jure Radića, T021-604300, www.osejava.com. Opened in summer 2009, this hotel has a cool minimalist interior and stands on the seafront, a 10-min walk from the main town beach. There are 40 rooms and 5 suites, each with an oversized photo of a landscape, seascape or cityscape covering an entire wall, and a slick bathroom with a glass door, making it visible from the bedroom. Facilities include 2 restaurants, an outdoor pool, and a wellness centre with gym, sauna and massage.

**€ Batosić Pansion**, Kipara Meštrovića 25, T021-612974, www.batosic.com. Just a 10-min walk uphill from the centre of town, this friendly, peaceful B&B has 10 spacious rooms with free Wi-Fi, balconies and en suite bathrooms. Breakfast is served on a covered garden patio and there's also a barbecue where guests can cook. The host spent 20 years in California and also offers yoga classes, sailing lessons and bikes to rent.

## Island of Brač *p68*
### Supetar

**€€€€ Hotel Bračka Perla**, Put Vele Luke 53, T021-755530, www.perlacroatia.com. Looking out onto a small bay, close to the centre of Supetar, this luxurious boutique hotel is built of natural stone and centres on a garden with a pool overlooking the sea. There are 5 rooms and 6 suites, all with wooden floors and colourful modern decor. Facilities include a small wellness centre and an adjoining farm producing wine, olive oil and cheese.

**€€ Hotel Villa Adriatica**, Put Vele Luka 31, T021-343806, www.villaadriatica.com. This family-run hotel is close to the main beach, and offers 24 rooms with balconies and bright, cheerful decor, plus a funky restaurant and a leafy garden with a cocktail bar and a small pool.

### Bol

**€€ Hotel Kaštil**, Frane Radića 1, T021-635995, www.kastil.hr. This old stone building overlooking the harbour offers 32 slick, minimalist-style guest rooms. It has its own restaurant, on a 1st-floor terrace above the sea, and a street-level pizzeria and cocktail bar.

**€€ Villa Giardino**, Novi put 2, T021-635900, no website. Open May-Oct. Set in lush gardens, a 5-min walk from the harbour, this cheerful, family-run B&B has 5 rooms furnished with antiques. Breakfast is served in the garden and the owner, who is a sculptor, is keen to share his home-made rajika with guests.

**€ Zlatni Bol Apartments**, Ivana Gundulica 2, T091-2244700, www.zlatni-bol.com. Just a 5-min walk from the centre, and a 20-min walk to Zlatni Rt beach, this carefully designed complex has 5 studios (sleeping 2-3) and four apartments (sleeping 4). Welcoming and peaceful, each unit comes with a kitchenette and a private terrace for sitting out.

## Island of Hvar *p69, map p70*
### Hvar Town

**€€€€ Hotel Riva**, Riva bb, T021-750100, www.suncanihvar.com. In an old stone building opposite the ferry quay, this hotel (formerly known as the Slavija) reopened in 2006 following total renovation. Now stunningly chic, the 46 rooms and 8 suites are decorated in minimalist style, in tones of grey and charcoal, with splashes of vibrant red. An amusing feature in each unit is the bathroom, which is visible from the bed through a glass wall. Out front, the Roots Restaurant and BB Club cocktail bar offer open-air seating on a large terrace overlooking the palm-lined waterfront.

**€€€ Hotel Podstine**, Pod Stine bb, T021-740400, www.podstine.com. Located on the coast, a 20-min walk west of the main square, this peaceful and luxurious family-run hotel has a lovely terrace restaurant by a pebble beach, backed by palms and pine trees. There are 40 rooms, each with a sea view, plus a wellness centre with a pool, gym, massage, sauna and beauty treatments.

**€€ Aparthotel Pharia**, Put Podstine 1, T021-778080, www.orvas-hotels.com. This friendly hotel lies on the coast, a pleasant 20-min walk west of town, near Hotel Podstine. There are 10 double rooms and 11 apartments, all with a/c, satellite TV and a balcony, while the apartments also have a kitchenette and living room. You pay a bit more for a sea view, but it's worth it. There's a bar but no restaurant.

**€€ Palmižana**, Sveti Klement, T021-717270, www.palmizana.hr. Palmižana lies on Sveti Klement, one of the Pakleni islets, and can reached by regular taxi-boat from Hvar Town. Set in grounds planted with pines, palms and exotic shrubs, this wonderful hideaway comprises 7 villas, 6 bungalows and 2 restaurants. Everything is built of local stone and beautifully designed to blend with the natural environment. Each unit has a funky interior painted in deep vibrant colours and decorated with contemporary artwork.

**€€ Villa Town Gate**, Hektorovićeva 1, T091-506 9888, www.villahvar.eu. For a central location you can't do much better than this – tucked away in a narrow cobbled street in the medieval old town, just off the main square. This renovated old stone building offers comfortable modern rooms with tile floors and 2 penthouse apartments, all with a/c, a fridge and free Wi-Fi.

**€ Green Lizard Hostel**, Hvar Town, T021-742560, www.greenlizard.hr. A 10-min walk from the seafront, this friendly hostel offers bunkbeds in dorms, plus 2 double rooms with en-suite bathrooms, and a BBQ in the garden.

**€ Hotel Fortuna**, Milna, T021-745021, fortuna-hvar.com. Right on the beach in peaceful Milna, 5 km from Hvar Town, this friendly family-run hotel has simple comfortable rooms with wooden floors, and a restaurant with a sea-view terrace. You get a generous breakfast, plus the chance of any early morning swim. They offer pick-up from Hvar Town if you don't have a car.

### Jelsa
**€€€ The Quaich**, Vrbanj, T021-768214, www.quaichexperience.co.uk. In Vrbanj, 4 km from Jelsa, this complex of old stone buildings has been carefully renovated to form three boho-chic cottages with self-catering facilities. There's a garden with an outdoor pool, grapevines, hammocks and a BBQ, and meals are served in a communal courtyard on request.

**€ Apartmani Grgičević**, Vitarnja, T097-7989777, www.croatiapartment.biz. A pleasant 15-min walk from the centre of Jelsa, in a peaceful part of town backed by pinewoods and overlooking the sea, this is great place to escape the crowds. There are 5 apartments, all with wooden floors, kitchenettes, free Wi-Fi and sea-view balconies. Guests also have the use of a BBQ in the garden.

### Island of Vis *p72*
### Vis Town
**€€ Hotel San Giorgio**, Petra Hektorovicà 2, Kut, T021-711362, www.hotelsangiorgiovis.com. Formerly known as Hotel Paula, this 10-room hotel is hidden away in an old stone building in a cobbled side street. As of 2009, the interior decor is slick, modern and minimalist and each room has a king-size bed and flat-screen TV. On the top floor there's a honeymoon suite with a terrace and jacuzzi. They have bikes to hire and can arrange massage and beauty treatments. Downstairs there's a small garden restaurant, with tables on a walled terrace.

**€ Pansion Dionis**, Matije Gubca 1, T021-711963, www.dionis.hr. This small B&B has 7 doubles and 1 triple, all with wooden floors, simple, modern, wooden furniture, a/c, satellite TV and en suite bathroom. Most units also have shared terraces overlooking the bay. Breakfast is served in the Pizza Bar Dionis, under the same management.

### Komiža
**€€ Villa Nonna**, Ribarska 50, T021-713500, www.villa-nonna.com. This old stone townhouse, overlooking the harbour, was renovated in 2005 to provide 7 bright and airy apartments, each named after a local plant and painted in appropriate shades. Expect wooden floors and some exposed stonework, a/c, satellite TV and a fully equipped kitchenette.

**€ Insula Apartments**, Dr. Ante Starčevića 27, T021-713029, www.insula-vis.com. In an old stone house just a 5-min walk from the centre, Insula offers 3 tastefully furnished apartments, plus a shared courtyard with a BBQ.

**€ Villa Kamenica**, Mihovila Pavlinovića 15, T099-8580696, www.villa-kamenica.hr. Just a 5-min walk from the harbour, this villa is set in a lush garden with lemon trees and lavender, a barbecue and a big outdoor table. There are 3 apartments, each with a/c, satellite TV, a fully equipped kitchenette and a furnished balcony. The owners are kind and helpful and full of local advice.

**Split** *p56, maps p56 and p60*
## Diocletian's Palace and the historic centre

**€€ Apetit,** Šubićeva 5, T021-332549, apetit-split.hr. In a side street between the main square and the seafront, **Apetit** occupies a 2nd-floor dining room with medieval stonework, modern furnishing and contemporary oil paintings. Come here for creative Dalmatian cooking – home-made pasta dishes, tuna steaks and colourful salads, all carefully presented. An excellent choice for a rainy day.

**€€ Kod Jose,** Sredmanuška 4, just outside the palace walls, close to Zlatna Vrata, T021-347397. This typical Dalmatian *konoba* combines rough stone walls, heavy wooden tables and candlelight. Top dishes are the risottos and fresh fish – the choice changes daily so you'll need to ask to see what's on offer. The discreet waiters deserve a special mention.

**€€ Konoba Matejuška,** Tomića stine 3, T021-355152, www.konobamatejuska.hr. This tiny eatery serves tasty fresh local seafood dishes and wine. There's a cosy dining room with stone walls, a wooden beamed ceiling, and just 6 tables, plus a few more small tables out front in the narrow side alley. Upstairs, in Villa Matejuška, they have apartments (see page 74).

**€€ Konoba Varoš,** Ban Mladenova 7, between the centre and Marjan, T021-396138, www.konobavaros.com. Less atmospheric than **Kod Jose** and **Konoba Matejuška**, though the risotto, fried squid and fresh fish are often even better here. The walls are decorated with seascapes and paintings of ships, and the ceiling hung with fishing nets. They have a few tables out front, on the street.

**€€ Restoran Jugo,** close to **Hotel Jadran**, between the gardens of Sveti Stipan and the ACI Marina, T021-398900. Worth the 15-min walk from the centre for its summer terrace with views of the marina, and a fantastic view of the city behind. Serves up passable Dalmatian dishes and pizza.

**€€ Šperun,** Šperun 3, T021-346999. In a side street between the Riva and Varoš, this cosy restaurant offers typical Dalmatian dishes such as *brodet* (fish stew), *bakalar* (dried cod) and *crni rižot* (risotto prepared in cuttlefish ink).

**€ Dioklecijan (Tri Volta),** Dosud 9, no phone. Known affectionately as Tri Volta, after the 3 arches on the terrace that form part of the palace walls, this bar is popular with local fishermen. You can get *merenda* here the year through: early morning helpings of hearty dishes such as *gulaš* (goulash) and *tripice* (tripe). During summer the menu is refined and extended to cater for tourists.

**€ Fife,** Trumbićeva obala 11, T021-345223. Overlooking Matejuška, where fishermen from Varoš keep their boats, this eatery is truly down-to-earth, though tourist now outnumber locals during summer. The menu changes daily: look out for *juha* (soup), *crni rižot* (risotto prepared with cuttlefish ink) and *palačinke* (pancakes).

**€ Makrovega,** Leština 2, T021-394440, www.makrovega.hr, Mon-Fri 0900-2000, Sat 0900-1700, Sun closed. Unusual for Croatia, this informal eatery specializes in vegetarian fare. You'll find it in **Varoš** (slightly hidden, but it is signed) doing daily set-menus (vegetarian and vegan options) plus soups, pasta dishes and salads. Everything is fresh and tasty.

**€ Pizzeria Galija,** Tončićeva 12, T021-347932. Close to the fish market, Galija reputedly does the best pizzas in town, plus pasta dishes and salads. The informal atmosphere and set up – wooden tables and benches, draught beer and wine by the glass – make it popular with locals the year through. It now has additional tables on a front terrace, with outdoor heaters in winter.

**€ Rizzo,** Tončićeva 6, T021-348349. Excellent sandwich bar, hidden away between the fish market and **Pizzeria Galija**. Oven-warm bread rolls are filled with cheese, salami, tuna and salad of your choice.

**€ Zlatna Ribica**, Kraj Sv Marije 8, T021-348710. May-Sep, Mon-Fri 0600-2100 and Sat 0600-1400, Oct-Apr Mon-Sat 0600-1400. This stand-up seafood eatery is directly next to the fish market, so everything on offer is guaranteed to be fresh. Try *girice* (small fried fish) or *frigane ligne* (fried squid), accompanied by a glass of *bevanda* (half white wine, half water).

### Cafés and bars

**Luxor**, Kraj Sv. Ivana 11, T021-341082, www.lvxor.hr. Ideal stopping place while sightseeing, on Peristil opposite the cathedral. They do light snacks as well as drinks, and even put cushions out so you can sit on the Roman steps. After-dark live music in summer.

**Vidilica**, Nazarov Prilaz 1, T021-394925. Above Varoš, on Marjan hill, the front terrace at this café affords amazing views over Split, the mountains, sea and islands.

**Žbirac**, Bačvice Bay. Overlooking Bačvica beach and much loved by locals, this low-key café has outdoor tables on a wooden deck shaded by tamarisk trees.

### Trogir *p64*

**€€ Čelica**, Čiovo bridge, T021-882344. Daily lunch and dinner. This old wooden car ferry, anchored by Čiovo bridge, has been converted to form an unusual restaurant. The owner catches and cooks the seafood, his speciality is *riblja juha* (fish soup).

**€€-€ Škrapa**, Hrvatskih mučenika 9, T021-885313. Daily lunch and dinner. Popular with both locals and visitors, Škrapa serves up large platters of delicious *frigne ligne* (fried squid) and *ribice* (small fried fish), as well other Dalmatian favourites. It's informal and fun, with heavy wooden tables and benches both indoors and out.

### Šibenik and around *p64*

**€€ Konoba Dalmatino**, Fra Nikole Ružiča 2, Šibenik, T091-542 4808. Daily lunch and dinner. In Šibenik's old town, this tiny old-fashioned eatery is a great spot for fresh fish and Dalmatian specialities such as *pršut* (prosciutto) and *sir* (cheese). It doubles as an upmarket wine shop.

**€€ Konoba Toni**, Dr. Franje Tuđmana 46, Skradin, T022-771177, www.konoba-toni-skradin.com. Daily lunch and dinner. On the edge of Krka National Park, this rustic *konoba* specializes in traditional Dalmatian dishes such as *brudet sa purom* (fish stew with polenta) prepared over an open fire, and lamb and veal cooked under a *peka*.

**€€ Pelegrini**, Jurja Dalmatinca 1, T022-213701, www.pelegrini.hr. Jun-Oct daily 1200-2400, Apr-May Tue-Sun 1200-2400, Nov-Mar Thu-Sat 1200-2400, Sun 1200-1800. On the square in front of the cathedral, this gourmet restaurant serves Creative Dalmatian cuisine – expect pasta with *pršut* (prosciutto), sheeps' cheese and truffles, and tuna sausages with lentils – plus an outstanding wine list (and sommelier). A little expensive, but worth it.

**€€ Zlatne Školjke**, Grgura Ninskog 9, Skradin, T022-771022, www.zlatne-skoljke.com. Daily lunch and dinner. On the edge of Krka National Park, in an old stone house with a summer terrace overlooking Skradin's ACI Marina, this restaurant is best known for *crni rižot* (black risotto), *špageti plodovima mora* (spaghetti with seafood) and *riba na žaru* (barbecued fish).

### Omiš *p66*

**€€ Radmanove Mlinice**, Cetina Valley, T021-862073, www.radmanove-mlinice.hr. Apr-Oct for lunch and dinner. On the banks of the River Cetina, 6 km upstream from Omiš, this old watermill was once the home of the Radman family. Today it's a pleasant garden restaurant serving local *pastrva* (trout) and *janjetina* (roast lamb) at tables under the trees.

### Makarska *p66*

**€€ Stari Mlin**, Prvosvibanjska 43, T021-611503. Mon-Sat for lunch and dinner, closed Sun. Housed in an 18th-century baroque building, a few blocks back from the seafront, Stari Mlin specializes in fish and seafood, plus a small selection of Thai dishes. The cavernous interior is warm and cosy through winter, while a large vine-covered terrace comes into use through summer.

**€€-€ Konoba Kalalarga**, Kalalarga 40, T098-9902908. Popular with locals, Kalalarga is a typical Dalmatian konoba, with exposed stonewalls, rustic wooden furniture and wine served by the carafe. The menu changes daily, normally comprising just 5-6 dishes, and is handwritten on a piece of paper – expect fried whitebait, seafood risotto and tuna steaks.

### Island of Brač p68
### Supetar

**€€ Kopačina**, Donji Humac, 8 km from Supetar, T021-647707, www.konoba-kopacina.com. Daily lunch and dinner. In the hill village of Donji Humac, this old-fashioned *konoba* is much loved by locals and manages to stay open all year. Most people come here especially to eat *janjetina* (roast lamb) at wooden tables and benches on a raised front terrace.

**€€ Vinotoka**, Jobova 6, T021-631341. Daily lunch and dinner. Said by locals to be one of the best restaurants on the island, Vinotoka is a couple of blocks back from the bay. Fresh fish and shellfish top the menu, with most dishes prepared outside on a *roštilj* (barbecue).

### Bol

**€€ Dalmatino**, Frane Radić 14, T091-5455779. Daily lunch and dinner. In an old stone building in the centre of Bol, this small restaurant (ex-Gušt) offers a good range of fish and lobster dishes, as well as *janjetina* (roast lamb) and *paštidaca* (beef stew). There are a few tables outside on the terrace, but you may have to queue for a seat.

**€€ Ribarska Kučica**, Ante Starčevića bb, T021-635033, www.ribarska-kucica.com. Jun-Sep for lunch and dinner. On the coastal path, a 10-min walk east of the crowds in the centre of Bol, this informal eatery serves

fresh fish, pasta and pizza at romantic, candlelit tables overlooking the open sea. There's also an adjoining cocktail bar under the same management.

### Island of Hvar p69, map p70
### Hvar Town

**€€ Giaxa**, Petra Hektorovića bb, T021-741073, www.giaxa.com. In the old town, this sophisticated candlelit restaurant opens onto a romantic stone courtyard with funky modern furnishing. The menu features creative Mediterranean cuisine – pasta and truffles, local seafood dishes with a twist, excellent wines and delicious desserts.

**€€ Luna**, Grod bb, T021-741400. On the 1st floor of a stone building in the old town, Luna's dining room has a large open space in the roof so you can see the sky and stars at night. Try the excellent fresh fish (they'll bring you a platter of uncooked fish so you can choose which one you want before it's cooked), while meat eaters might opt for chicken with truffles, or a steak.

**€€ Macondo**, Groda bb, T021-742850. This excellent fish restaurant is in a narrow alleyway between the main square and the fortress. In summer there are several tables outside, while the indoor space has a large open fire and is hung with discreet modern art. Start with scampi pâté, followed by a platter of mixed fried fish, and round it off with a glass of home-made *orahovica* (*rakija* made from walnuts). The food and service are practically faultless, but you may have to queue for a table.

**€ Alviž**, Dolac bb, T021-742797, www.hvar-alviz.com. This friendly, family-run pizzeria occupies an old stone building behind the cathedral, opposite the bus station. The shabby-chic interior with whitewashed stone walls opens onto a lovely peaceful courtyard garden with grape vines. Besides pizzas they also do excellent *palačinke* (crêpes).

**€ Konoba Menego**, Groda bb, T021-742036, www.menego.hr. On the steps leading up to the castle, this informal eatery and wine bar serves small platters of locally produced

Dalmatian specialities such as *kožji sir* (goat's cheese), *pršut* (prosciutto) and *salata od hobotnice* (octopus salad), plus carafes of home-made wine. Typical of a *konoba*, it has exposed stone walls, a wooden-beamed ceiling and candlelit tables.

## Stari Grad

**€€ Jurin Podrum**, Donja kola bb, T021-765448. Still a local favourite, this rustic stonewalled eatery has half a dozen tables outside in the narrow alleyway. Come here for Dalmatian cooking with a twist – expect tasty dishes such as octopus stew with grilled polenta, pasta with chicken and figs, and a sublime chocolate mousse. The portions are generous and the service friendly but professional.

**€€ Stari Mlin**, Iza škole, T021-765804 TIC list – T091-5736376. Opened in 2008 by owner-chef Damir Cavić, who used to run the very popular Jurin Podrum, this excellent family-run eatery occupies a traditional stone building in the old town. The menu features fresh local fish and seafood. It's popular with locals as well as visitors who arrive by yacht, and stays open all year.

## Jelsa

**€€ Konoba Humac**, Humac, 8 km east of Jelsa, T021-768108 and T091-5239463. Jun-Sep Mon-Sat for lunch and dinner. There's no electricity so everything is cooked as it would have been over a century ago: under a *peka* or on a *roštilj*. The octopus is exceptional, the bread home-made and the cheese, salad and wine locally produced. You can't get much more authentic than this.

**€€ Me & Mrs Jones**, Mala Banda, T091-7363354. Looking out over the harbour, this gourmet eatery (ex-Napoleon) serves up creative Mediterranean cuisine, with an emphasis on fresh local fish such as sea bass and tuna. The stone-walled dining room is candle-lit by night, and outdoor tables line the water's edge.

## Island of Vis *p72*
## Vis Town

**€€ Lola**, Mate Gupca 12, T095-8497932, www.lolavisisland.com. Run by a Croatian-Spanish couple, this colourful eatery lies in a garden with lemon trees. The menu combines fresh Dalmatian ingredients with a little extra flare from Spain and Morocco, so you can expect dishes such as gazpacho, coucous salad, and trout with beetroot risotto, plus delicious deserts.

**€€ Pojoda**, Don Cvjetka Marasovic 8, T021-711575. Hidden away in a courtyard garden, this is a fine spot to taste local seafood specialities such as *salata od hobotnice* (octopus salad) and *brodet* (fish stew) along with a carafe of house wine. Round it all off with *rožata*, a Dubrovnik speciality similar to crème caramel.

**€€ Villa Kaliopa**, V Nazora 32, Kut, T021-711755. Close to the Town Museum, this enchanting but rather expensive restaurant is set in the romantic walled garden of a Renaissance villa. The menu changes daily, depending on what fresh products are available. Dinner here is an event in itself, and worth dressing up for.

## Komiža

**€€ Konoba Bako**, Gundulićeva 1, T021-713742, www.konobabako.hr. Dinner only. This informal and friendly seafood restaurant is in a tiny bay with tables right up to the water's edge. The indoor dining area has rough stone walls and a pool stocked with fresh fish and lobster. The former Croatian president, Stjepan Mesić, has eaten here.

**€€ Konoba Jastožera**, Gundulićeva 6, T021-713859, www.jastozera.com. Opened in 2002, this restaurant is based in the former town lobster-pot house. The interior has been beautifully refurbished with tables set on wooden platforms above the water, and small boats can still enter the central space. Needless to say, the house speciality is lobster.

## 🄵 Bars and clubs

**Split** *p56, maps p56 and p60*

**Fluid**, Dosud 1. A tiny, cosy, stone-walled late-night drinking den, popular with both locals and visitors.

**Galerija Plavac**, Trg braće Radiča (down a narrow passageway off Marulićeva ). Bar staging temporary exhibitions by local artists and occasional live music, tables indoors and outside in a small internal courtyard.

**Ghetto Club**, Dosud 10. The alternative crowd meet here for drinks, occasional exhibitions and performances. Throughout the summer it gets incredibly busy, when tables spill outside onto a delightful candlelit courtyard and there is DJ music.

**Hemingway**, VIII Mediteranskih igara 5, T099-211 9993, www.hemingway.hr. Open daily; Fri and Sat until 0500. Opened in summer 2008, Split's Hemingway is part of a chain of pricey clubs, which started out in North Croatia. Attracting the see-and-be-seen crowd, it has a big summer terrace overlooking Poljud Marina. Expect guest DJs from abroad and a good mix of dance, disco, 1970s and house music.

**Ovčice**, Put Firule 4, T021-489759. A 5-min walk along the coast from Bačvice Bay, this pleasant sea-view terrace café stays open until 0300 in summer, with occasional guest DJ's and live music. During the day, you can hire an umbrella and sunlounger on the pebble beach.

### Northwest of Split *p64*

**Aurora Club**, Kamenar bb, Primošten (20 km southeast of Šibenik), T098-9201964, www.auroraclub.hr. Mid-Jun to early Sep. One of the largest discos in Dalmatia.

**Hacienda**, Magistrala bb, on the road between Šibenik and Vodice, T099-3332333, haciendaclub.eu. Jun-Sep. The biggest nightclub for miles, in a walled garden out of town.

### Southeast of Split *p66*

**Beach Bar Buba**, Donja Luka beach, Makarska, www.bubabar.com. Open May-Oct. On the main town beach, a 10-min walk west of the centre, during the day Buba hires out sunloungers and umbrellas, then plays electronic and dance music come sunset, with occasional live concerts.

**Deep**, Šetalište Fra Jure Radića bb, Osejava Peninsula, Makarska, www.deep.hr. Open Jun-Sep. A small summer bar and disco, in a natural cave overlooking the sea, playing electronic music with laser shows. It is a 10-min walk east of the centre, just after Hotel Osejava.

**Grotta**, Šetalište Sv Petra bb, Makarska. Open Jun-Sep. A long-standing small bar and nightclub, playing rock and dance music, in a natural cave overlooking the sea on St Peter's peninsula, with amazing views back to town across the bay.

**Petar Pan**, Fra Jure Radića bb, Makarska, www.petarpan-makarska.com. Open Jul-Aug. At the south end of the seafront promenade, this open-air disco has a sophisticated sound and light system and space for 1500 guests. It attracts visiting electro dance DJs such as DJs from Mars a Latin Prince.

### Island of Brač *p68*

**Varadero**, Frane Radić 1, Bol. On the ground floor of Hotel Kaštil, close to the harbour, this cocktail bar pulls the crowds through summer and hosts occasional guest DJs.

### Island of Hvar *p69, map p70*

**Carpe Diem**, Riva bb, Hvar Town, T021-717234, www.carpe-diem-hvar.com. Open until 0300 in the peak season. Trendy cocktail bar with oriental furniture and a plant-filled summer terrace looking out to sea. Through peak season it's literally packed and they have bouncers outside. A bit pretentious, but a great venue for celebrity spotting, if that's your thing.

**Hula Hula**, Hvar Town, on the seaside path between Hotel Amfora and Hotel Podstine, www.hulahulahvar.com. Daily Jun-Sep. This wooden beach bar makes the perfect spot to watch the sunset with chill-out music and a drink, in a small pebble cove looking out to sea.

**Kiva**, Hvar Town, in a narrow side street off the harbor, kivabarhvar.com. Apr-Oct 2100-0300. This tiny, informal wine bar plays classic rock and alternative music. Popular with young Croatians and hard-drinking sailing types; once it's full inside customers spill out onto the street. It can get a bit rowdy when the Australian backpackers arrive.

**The Top**, Fabrika bb, Hvar Town. On the top floor of Hotel Adriana, this stunning rooftop lounge-bar affords views over the old town and out to sea. Tables and lounge sofas are arranged on a series of multi-level garden terraces. Chic but informal, it serves cocktails, wine and light snacks through the day and into the early hours.

**Veneranda**, Gornja cesta bb, Hvar Town, T098-855151, www.veneranda.hr. Open Jun-Sep. Above the coastal path west of town, in the grounds of a former 16th-century Greek Orthodox Monastery, this complex includes a cocktail bar (in the former church), a pool and a dance floor playing techno and electronic music. Prince Harry brought it to the attention of the gossip magazines, when he fell into the pool in 2011.

## Island of Vis *p72*
**Aquarius**, Kamenica Beach (a 10-min walk east of the harbour), Komiža. Open Jun-Sep. This tiny beach bar offers sunloungers, umbrellas and chill-out music by day, followed by house, dance and electronic music with drinks at night.

**Lambik**, Kut, Vis Town, T 091-1681952. Popular with the yachting crowd for a pre-dinner aperitif, this bar serves coffee, local wines, slightly pricey cocktails and snacks the day through in a lovely 17th-century stone courtyard.

## ⚙ Festivals

**Split** *p56, maps p56 and p60*
**7 May  Sudamje**, The Feast of St Domnius celebrates the patron saint of Split, whose bones go on display for a week in the cathedral. It's a local public holiday. Stands sell handmade wooden objects and basketry.
**Jul-Aug  Split Sumer Festival**, www.splitsko-ljeto.hr. Hosts opera, theatre and dance, with the main stage on Prokurativo, between Varoš and Diocletian's Palace.

### Around Split *p63*
**Late Jul  Ethnoambient Salona**, Salona, www.ethnoambient.net. A 3-day open-air event attracting musicians from as far afield as Scotland, Portugal and Greece.

### Šibenik *p64*
**Mid-Aug, Terraneo**, terraneofestival.com. This world-class 4-day alternative music festival sees an international line-up – Groove Armada and The Swans played here in summer 2012, The Fall and Nouvelle Vaugue in 2011.

## 🛍 Shopping

**Split** *p56, maps p56 and p60*
**Books**
**Algoritum**, Bajamontijeva 2, between Peristil and Narodni Trg, T021-348030. The best bookshop for foreign-language publications, including novels, travel guides and maps.

**Clothes**
**Think Pink**, Zadarska 8, T021-317126, www.thinkpink.com.hr. This boutique stocks unusual and innovative clothing, shoes and jewellery crated by young Croatian designers. They have a second slightly smaller store at Kružiæeva 6, T021-341061.

## Food and drink

**Pazar**, colourful open-air market just outside the palace walls, with stalls selling fruit and vegetables, plus clothes and leather goods.

## Souvenirs

**Croata**, Krešmirova 11, T021-314055, www.croata.hr. Sells original Croatian ties in presentation boxes, with a history of the tie.

## ⚓ What to do

**Split and around** *p56, maps p56 and p60*
### Adventure sports
**Adventure Dalmatia**, Matije Gupca 26, Split, T021-540642, www.adventuredalmatia.com. Arranges rafting, canoeing, canyoning and free climbing in the Cetina Valley near Omiš, and sea kayaking in Trogir and Brela.
**Dalmatia Trekking**, T098-1962620, dalmatiatrekking.com. Organizes 1-day and multi-day guided hiking expeditions on the islands of Vis and Hvar, as well as up Biokovo and down the Cetina Valley.

## Sailing
**Ultra Sailing**, Uvala baluni bb, T021-398578, www.ultra-sailing.hr. Arranges yacht charters, as well as the Ultra Sailing School in Trogir, Apr-Oct, with 1-week courses at basic and advanced levels.

**Northwest of Split** *p64*
### Adventure sports
**Nik**, A Šupuka 5, T022-338550, Šibenik, www.nik.hr. Arranges excursions by boat from Šibenik to the nearby national parks of Krka and Kornati.

**Southeast of Split** *p66*
### Adventure sports
**Active Holidays**, Knezova Kačića bb, Omiš, T021-861829, www.activeholidays-croatia.com. Organizes rafting, canoeing, free-climbing, paragliding, windsurfing and sea-kayaking in Omiš and the surrounding area.
**Biokovo Active Holidays**, Kralja P Krešimira IV 7B, Makarska, T021-679655, www.biokovo.

net. Organizes 1-day and several-day adventure sports programmes including hiking and mountain biking on Biokovo and the island of Brač, rafting on the Cetina and sea kayaking at Brela.

## Diving
**More-Sub**, Kralja P Krešimira 43, Makarska, T021-611727, www.more-sub-makarska.hr.

**Island of Brač** *p68*
### Adventure sports
**Big Blue**, Podan Glavice 2, Bol, T021-635614, www.big-blue-sport.hr. Arranges scuba-diving, wind-surfing and sea kayaking at Zlatni Rat, and rents out mountain bikes.
**Big Blu Diving**, Bračka cesta 13, Bol, T098-425496, www.big-blue-diving.hr.

## Diving
**Amber Dive Center**, Supetar, T098-922 7512, www.amber-divecenter.com.

**Island of Hvar** *p69, map p70*
### Adventure sports
**Hvar Adventure**, Obala bb, Hvar Town, T021-717813, www.hvar-adventure.com. Sea-kayaking tours, sailing expeditions, hiking, cycling and rock climbing.

## Diving
**Diving Center Viking**, Podstine bb, T021-742529, www.viking-diving.com.

## Spas and retreats
**Hvareno**, Dol, 6 km from Jelsa, T021-765635, www.hvareno.com. Hvareno offers yoga (Shadow Yoga) and overnight accommodation, excellent breakfast and an optional evening meal.
**Sensori Spa**, Hotel Adriana, T021-750250, www.suncanihvar.com. A luxurious wellness centre comprising an indoor rooftop pool filled with heated seawater, plus a selection of massage treatments, facials and aromatherapy.
**Suncokret**, Dol, T091-739 2526, www.suncokretdream.net. Also in Dol, **Suncokret**

(Sunflower) offers holistic wellness retreats combining yoga, nature walks and reiki, plus accommodation.

## Island of Vis *p72*
### Adventure sports
**Alternatura**, Hrvatskih Mučenika 2, Komiža, T021-717239, www.alternatura.hr. Activities and tours such as boat trips to the Blue Cave on Biševo, as well as free climbing, paragliding, caving, sea-kayaking and sailing.

### Diving
**Dodoro Diving Tours**, Trg Klapavica 1, Vis Town, T091-251 2263, www.dodoro-diving.com.
**Issa Diving Centre**, Ribarska 91, Komiža, T021-713651, www.scubadiving.hr.

## ⊖ Transport

See also Transport in Dubrovnik and South Dalmatian Coast, page 10.

**Split** *p56, maps p56 and p60*
### Bus
From Split, frequent buses run to **Šibenik** (1½ hrs), **Makarska** (1½ hrs), **Rijeka** (7 hrs), **Pula** (10 hrs), **Dubrovnik** (4 hrs) and **Zagreb** (5-7 hrs, depending on the route).

### Train
From Split there are daily trains to **Zagreb** (5½ hrs by day; 8 hrs by night).

## ❶ Directory

**Split** *p56, maps p56 and p60*
**Hospital** Hospital Firule, Spinčićeva 1, a 15-min walk east of the centre, T021-556111 (24-hr casualty). **Pharmacy** Each pharmacy is marked by a glowing green cross. Ljekarna Dobri (Gundilićeva 52, T021-348074) and Ljekarna Lučac (Pupačićeva 4, T021-533188) are reasonably central and work alternate 24-hr shifts.

**Šibenik and around** *p64*
**Hospital** Šibenik hospital, Stjepana Radića 83, a 15-min walk southeast of the centre, T022-246246. Ljekarna Centrala, Stjepana Radića bb (T022-213539) and Ljekarna Varoš, Kralja Zvonimira 32 (T022-212249) are central and work alternate 24-hr shifts.

**Island of Brač** *p68*
**Hospital** The nearest hospital is in Split back on the mainland. **Pharmacy** You will find pharmacies in Supetar (T021-757308) and Bol (T021-635987).

**Island of Hvar** *p69, map p70*
**Hospital** The nearest hospital is in Split on the mainland. **Pharmacy** You will find pharmacies in Hvar Town (T021-741002), Stari Grad (T021-765061) and Jelsa (T021-761108).

**Island of Vis** *p72*
**Hospital** The nearest hospital is in Split, on the mainland. **Pharmacy** There are pharmacies in Vis Town (T021-711434) and Komiža (T021-713445).

## Contents

## Footprint features

North Dalmatian Coast

**Zadar** → *For listings, see pages 94-98.*

Sitting compact on a rectangular peninsula, accessible only to pedestrians, the historic centre of Zadar is renowned throughout Croatia for its beautiful medieval churches, the most impressive being St Donat, which stands on the site of the ancient Roman forum. Close by, in the St Mary's Convent complex, the Gold and Silver of Zadar exhibition is a stunning collection of minutely detailed Byzantine reliquaries. The narrow cobbled streets are lined with fine Venetian-style town houses, many converted into shops and cafés at ground level, giving the old town the buzz of a modern-day urban centre. The surrounding modern suburbs are dispersed and more difficult to negotiate: most of the big resort hotels, restaurants and sports facilities lie 5 km along the coast at Puntamika and Borik. All the sights listed here are in Zadar's old town and are within walking distance of one another.

# Zadar

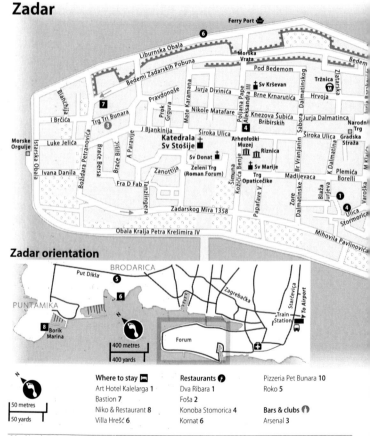

## Zadar orientation

| Where to stay 🛏 | Restaurants 🍴 | Pizzeria Pet Bunara 10 |
|---|---|---|
| Art Hotel Kalelarga 1 | Dva Ribara 1 | Roko 5 |
| Bastion 7 | Foša 2 | |
| Niko & Restaurant 8 | Konoba Stomorica 4 | Bars & clubs 🍸 |
| Villa Hrešč 6 | Kornat 6 | Arsenal 3 |

## Arriving in Zadar

**Getting there** Zadar Airport ① *T023-205800, www.zadar-airport.hr* is 8 km east of the city centre and is served by shuttle bus (25Kn). The **bus station** is on ① *Ante Starčevića 2, T023-211555, www.liburnija-zadar.hr*. **Jadrolinija** ① *www.jadrolinija.hr*, runs a ferry service from Zadar to Mali Lošinj (Kvarner), stopping at several smaller islands en route. It also operates daily local ferries to nearby islands. **Emilia Romagna Lines** ① *www.emiliaromagnalines.it*, run a catamaran between Zadar and Cesenatico and Pesaro (Italy), in August only. The train station is next to the **bus station** ① *T060-333444 (national train information) www.hznet.hr*.

**Tourist information** Zadar city tourist office at ① *Ilije Smiljanića bb, T023-212222, www.tzzadar.hr*. There's a walk-in **tourist information centre** at ① *Mihovila Klaića 1, T023-316166*. The **regional tourist office** at is ① *Leopolda Mandića 1, T023-315316, www.zadar.hr*.

## Forum

The Romans founded Zadar as Jadera, and developed it into a port and fortified market town with a forum, theatre and public baths). Now known as Zeleni Trg, the ancient forum dates from between the first century BC and the third century AD. In Roman times it served as the main market place and public meeting space; still today the city's top monuments, floodlit at night, are found here. On the northwest corner stands an ancient Roman column used as a 'pole of shame' from the Middle Ages up until 1840, where criminals were chained and exposed to public scorn and ridicule.

## Crkva Sv Donat

① *Zeleni Trg. Apr-Sep 0900-1400 and 1700-2100, Oct-Mar 0900-1400.*

Following the fall of the Western Roman Empire in the fifth century, Zadar became the capital of the Byzantine *thema* (province) of Dalmatia. Standing in the centre of the Forum, the ninth-century Church of St Donat dates from that period. An imposing rotonda, it's Zadar's best-known monument and the largest Byzantine building in Croatia. Standing 27 m high, it's a robust cylindrical structure flanked by three circular apses. Fragments of Roman stones have been incorporated into the sturdy outer walls, and inside a matroneum (womens' gallery) is supported by six pilasters and two Roman columns, and capped by a central dome. St Donat

## Maraschino

While in Zadar, be sure to try Maraschino, a bittersweet syrupy liquor made from Marasca cherries and manufactured here since 1821. Its unique almond flavour is obtained by crushing the cherry stones, and it can be drunk straight or mixed in cocktails. Through the decades it has been exported far and wide and is said to have won the hearts of world figures such as Napoleon and Queen Victoria.

ceased to function as a church during the early 19th century. Today it stands empty, but due to its excellent acoustics it hosts the annual summer festival of medieval, Renaissance and baroque music.

### Katedrala Sv Stošije

ⓘ *Zeleni Trg. Cathedral open daily. Bell-tower Jul-Aug 0900-2400, Jun and Sep 0900-2200, Apr-May and Oct 1000-1700, Nov-Mar closed, 10Kn. If you have a head for heights it's well worth climbing to the top of the cathedral's bell tower for spectacular views over the city.*

Next to Sv Donat stands the 12th-century, late Romanesque Cathedral of St Anastasia. Built on a rectangular ground plan, it has a splendid façade bearing three doors, a series of blind arches and two central rose windows, the lower one Romanesque and the upper one Gothic. Inside, you'll find a stone altar and wooden choir stalls from the 15th century. At the end of the left aisle, a smaller altar displays a ninth-century stone casket containing the remains of St Anastasia, to whom the cathedral is dedicated. Work on the bell tower began in the 15th century, though the upper three floors weren't completed until 1892 to drawings by the English architect TG Jackson.

### Arheološki Muzej

ⓘ *Trg Opatice Čike 1, T023-250516, www.amzd.hr. Apr-Sep 0900-1400, 1700-2100, Oct-Mar 0900-1400, 20Kn.*

Housed in a modern concrete building close to the Forum, the Archaeological Museum traces local history from the Stone Age to the late Middle Ages. The ground floor is devoted to finds from between the seventh and 12th centuries, and includes several fine examples of medieval stone carving. The first floor examines North Dalmatia under the Romans, while the second floor is given over to the Palaeolithic, Neolithic, Copper, Bronze and Iron Ages.

### Zlato i Srebro Zadra

ⓘ *Trg Opatice Čike 1, T023-250496. Mon-Sat 1000-1300, 1800-2000, Sun 1000-1200, 20 Kn.*

Standing next door to the early Romanesque Church of St Mary, the treasury houses a stunning collection known as *Zlato i Srebro Zadra* (Gold and Silver of Zadar), curated by the Benedictine nuns who live in the neighbouring Convent of St Mary.

The first floor displays a hoard of sumptuous reliquaries – arms and legs of various saints, encased in minutely detailed gold plating – and gold and silver processional crosses. On the second floor you'll find an equally well-displayed collection of religious paintings – look out for three panels from a 15th-century polyptych by the Venetian artist Vittore Carpaccio (1455-1526) and a striking Assumption of the Virgin from 1520 by Lorenzo Luzzo.

### Muzej antičkog stakla

① *Poljana Zemaljskog Odbora 1, T023-363831, www.mas-zadar.hr. Jun-Sep daily 0900-2100, Oct-May Mon-Sat 0900-1600, Sun closed. 30Kn.*

Opened in 2011, the Museum of Ancient Glass displays an impressive collection of Roman glassware, including sacred goblets and vessels for essential oils, found at archaeological sites throughout Dalmatia. There's a glass-blowing workshop and a small store selling replicas of museum exhibits. You'll find it in the 19th-century Cosmacendi Palace, on the edge of the old town.

### Morske Orgulje

① *Obala Kralja Petra Krešimira IV.*

On the tip of the old town peninsula, the extraordinary Sea Organ is made up of 35 pipes forming whistles that are played by the sea. The notes produced depend on the size of the waves, with the sea's energy creating ever-changing sounds. It was designed by Nikola Bašić and installed in 2005.

### Zadarski Pozdrav Suncu

① *Obala Kralja Petra Krešimira IV.*

Set into the stone-paved waterfront, next to the Sea Organ, the Greeting to the Sun is a 22-m circle made up of 300 multi-layered glass plates. Below the glass, light-sensitive solar modules absorb the sun's energy during the day, then transform it into electrical energy. Just after sunset, the lighting elements create an impressive light show, in harmony with the sounds of the Sea Organ. The pavement lights up in shades of blue, green, red and yellow, and local children meet here and race around chasing the light patterns. The solar modules can produce 46.500 kW per year – this energy is used for the Greeting to the Sun installation and for lighting the rest of the waterfront. It was installed in 2008 and, like the Sea Organ, was created by local architect Nikola Bašić.

### Narodni Trg

The People's Square took over the role of the Forum as the city's main square in the 16th century. On the west side stands the City Guardhouse, dating from 1562, with an imposing 18th-century clock tower. On the opposite side of the square, the 16th-century Renaissance loggia now houses an **art gallery** ① *T023-251851, Mon-Sat 0800-2000, Sun 0900-1300.*

---

## Island of Pag → *For listings, see pages 94-98.*

Long and skinny, rocky and barren, Pag's sparse pastures, scented with wild sage, support sheep farming, an important industry here, with twice as many sheep on the island as people. The island is known throughout the country for its *paški sir* (Pag cheese, made from sheep's milk) and *janjetina* (roast lamb). Several fertile valleys are given over to vineyards, producing two dry white wines, the golden-coloured Žutica and the light, crisp Gegić.

The chief settlement is the 15th-century Pag Town, with a long tradition of salt production and lacemaking, while the main tourist destination is the less appealing town of Novalja, a seaside resort with some decent pebble beaches and a string of late-night dance clubs, which also stage music festivals.

Note that while the southern half of Pag is considered North Dalmatia, the northern half officially belongs to the Kvarner region. However, to simplify the matter, the entire island is included in North Dalmatia here.

## Arriving on the island of Pag

**Getting there** Being joined to the mainland by a bridge at its southern tip, Pag is served by frequent buses from Zadar. **Pag Town bus station** is 500 m from the old town. **Novalja bus station** ① *T053-661500*, lies 500 m from the centre of town (bus information for both Novalja and Pag Town). In addition, **Jadrolinija** ① *www.jadrolinija.hr*, runs daily ferries from Rijeka in the Kvarner region to Novalja (northern tip of Pag), stopping at Rab Town (island of Rab) en route.

**Tourist information** ① *Trg Petra Krešimira IV, Pag Town, T023-611286, www.tzpag.hr, and Novalja, Trg Brišæiæ 1, T053-661404, www.tz-novalja.hr.*

## Pag Town

Located at the end of Pag Bay, Pag Town has been the island's capital since the 15th century. Its wealth was based on salt production and the salt pans can still be seen here today. Although there are no notable beaches, and the surrounding landscape is somewhat dreary, the old town is a gem of Renaissance architecture.

In 1443, while under Venetian rule, plans were drawn up to build a new fortified town, to defend against the Turks. The renowned architect Juraj Dalmatinac (also responsible for Šibenik Cathedral, see page 65) masterminded the project, which took several decades to build. A grid of narrow streets, centring on a main square with a cathedral and Rector's Palace, were to be enclosed by sturdy walls and 10 towers.

Today, apart from the walls, the complex remains intact. On the main square, Trg Kralja Petra Krešimira IV, stands the 15th-century Church of St Mary. Although it was never awarded the status of cathedral, it remains a proud monument based on the form of a three-nave Romanesque basilica, with a fine façade featuring a Renaissance rose window above an elegant Gothic portal. Café life centres on the main square, while much of the post-1960s tourist development such as hotels, apartments and restaurants lie west of town, overlooking a family beach, with shallow water suitable for kids.

## Novalja

Connected to Pag Town by daily buses, Novalja lies 21 km northwest of Pag Town in a sheltered cove backed by pinewoods, and is Pag's largest and busiest resort. Best known as party and clubbing destination, its not particularly attractive, but sees a constant flow of young holiday-makers through summer. Pristine, clear, emerald seawater and a number of bays with fine pebble beaches make it the best place for sunbathing on the island, while sports and late-night dance clubs compensate in part for its lack of cultural attractions.

The most popular bathing areas are the pebble beaches of Zrče, 2 km northeast of Novalja (served by shuttle bus in July and August), and Straško, a short walk south of Novalja town centre. Both are equipped with watersports facilities, showers, sun beds and umbrellas for hire, lifeguards, bars and eateries. Zrče beach has a special 24-hour licence, meaning that its bars and clubs can work non-stop, making it the only place of its kind in Croatia.

---

## Paklenica National Park → *For listings, see pages 94-98.*

Lying on the southeast slopes of the Velebit mountain chain, Paklenica National Park runs for 20 km along the Riviera, combining coastal and mountain scenery, which makes it it a haven for hikers and free-climbers. The lower levels are covered with beech forests, which give way to pines, dramatic rocky outcrops, mountain meadows and scree slopes. A refuge for wildlife, bears and wild boars are sighted in the more remote areas of Velebit.

## Arriving in Paklenica National Park

The best starting point for exploring the park is the seaside town of Starigrad Paklenica, overlooking the narrow Velebitski Kanal (Velebit Channel). Here, in the **Paklenica National Park** office ① *Tudjmana 14a, Starigrad Paklenica (42 km north of Zadar), T023-369202, www.paklenica.hr, May-Sep 50Kn, Oct-Apr 40Kn*, at the entrance to the park, you can pick up hiking maps and information about mountain refuges.

## Hiking in Paklenica National Park

The most popular walking route leads up the impressive limestone gorge of Velika Paklenica, which is 10 km long and up to 400 m deep, and runs from the highest peaks down to the sea. The path starts about 4 km inland from the park entrance at Starigrad Paklenica. Passing a couple of mountain refuges, a stiff climb will bring you to the 1757-m peak of Vaganski Vrh, the highest point on southern Velebit, offering stunning views over the sea and islands. This walk requires an entire day, and you should only set out armed with good hiking boots and a plentiful supply of water. Alternatively, a little way up the gorge, a secondary path branches off to the right, leading to Anića Kuk, a bizarre 721-m vertical rock form and a popular training ground for free-climbers. From here the path continues, passing through a dense forest, and eventually arrives at a height of 550 m, where you will find Manita Peč, a 500-m-long illuminated cave, filled with stalactites and stalagmites, which can be visited as part of a guided tour (ask at the national park office for details). A final stretch of path brings you to the 800 m peak of Vidakov Kuk.

Birdwatchers should note that rock partridges are often spotted on Paklenica's stony slopes, while birds of prey such as peregrine falcons and golden eagles may be sighted in Velika Paklenica gorge.

## River Zrmanja

The River Zrmanja is a typical karst river – its source lies in the Velebit mountains and it flows down to the Adriatic Sea. Its emerald-blue waters run 64 km, passing through valleys and magnificent steep-sided canyons, and over waterfalls and rapids en route. Various agencies (see page 98) arrange rafting, kayaking and canoeing here. A popular stretch for these tours lies between the villages of Kaštel Zegarski (15 km from Starigrad Paklnecia) and Muškovci, between which the river passes through a dramatic canyon.

# Kornati National Park → *For listings, see pages 94-98.*

## Tourist information
① *Kornati National Park office Butina 2, Murter, T022-435740, www.kornati.hr.*

## Visiting Kornati National Park

If you visit the park as part of an organized group, the entrance fee will be included in the price of the trip. If you're travelling by private boat, you pay depending on the size of your vessel. This can be done at any one of a number of kiosks scattered through the park (in June to September), from the national park head office in Murter (all year), or from nearby marinas.

Although the Kornati are best explored by private sailing boat, they can also be visited as part of an organized day trip, arranged by private agencies operating from nearby coastal resorts including Zadar and Šibenik (see pages 98 and 84 respectively).

Parallel to the mainland coast midway between Zadar and Šibenik, Kornati National Park covers an area 35 km long and 13 km wide, containing 89 islands, islets and reefs.

Declared a national park due to its wealth of underwater life and its unique natural beauty, the area is made up of crystal-clear blue sea and a scattering of eerie 'moonscape' islands supporting scanty vegetation.

Having no fresh water sources and little fertile land, the Kornati passed through the centuries with minimum human intervention. During the 17th century, noble families from Zadar, with the blessing of the Venetians, used the islands for sheep rearing, employing serfs from Murter as shepherds. Later, the Murterini bought rights to 90% of the Kornati, and continued to use them for seasonal farming: grazing sheep, cultivating olives, grapes and figs and keeping bees (there are few wild animals here other than lizards). They also built some 300 simple stone cottages, mainly in sheltered coves, which they used as temporary homes when fishing or tending the land. Today many of these cottages, still without running water and electricity, have been turned over to tourism, and are available for rent through the summer months, often with a small boat included, as 'Robinson Crusoe' retreats (see Where to stay, page 95).

## North Dalmatian Coast listings

*For hotel and restaurant price codes and other relevant information, see pages 12-19.*

### 🛏 Where to stay

**Zadar** *p88, map p88*

**€€€ Art Hotel Kalelarga**, Ulica Majke Margarite 3, T023-233000, www.arthotel-kalelarga.com. Superbly situated in the car-free old town, this boutique hotel has 10 rooms, with modern furnishing, wooden floors, some exposed medieval stonework and fantastic bathrooms, plus a gourmet restaurant.

**€€€ Hotel Bastion**, Bedemi zadarskih pobuna 13, T023-494950, www.hotel-bastion.hr. This stylish 4-star boutique hotel is ideally located, right in the heart of the old town, near the sea. It has 23 rooms and 5 suites, all with wooden floors and modern 'baroque' furnishing, plus shiny marble-and-tile bathrooms. Breakfast includes a buffet and cooked-to-order sausages, omelettes and pancakes. The staff are exceptionally friendly, and there's a small wellness centre, a restaurant, free parking and free Wi-Fi. It is a little pricey, but worth it.

**€€ Central Royal Apartments**, T091-2912978, www.centralroyalapartments.com. With 9 tastefully furnished self-catering apartments (mostly sleeping 2+2) at various locations within the old town, this makes a fine option to hotel accommodation while staying in Zadar.

**€€ Hotel Niko**, Obala Kneza Domagoja 9, Puntamika-Borik, T023-337880, www.hotel-niko.hr. What started out as the excellent **Restaurant Niko** (see Restaurants, page 95) with a romantic waterside terrace, now also has 12 guest rooms. Elegantly furnished with reproduction antiques, plush red carpets and sweeping curtains, each room has a/c, minibar and satellite TV. It's a 10-min drive (or a 45-min walk) from the Old Town.

**€ Villa Hrešč**, Obala kneza Trpimira 28, T023-337570, www.villa-hresc.hr. This modern pink villa has been renovated to form a luxurious establishment with 6 spacious apartments and 2 rooms. It's on the coast, offering a view of the old town across the water. Facilities include an upmarket restaurant and a garden with a pool.

### Island of Pag *p91*

**€€€ Hotel Pagus**, Ante Starčevića 1, Pag Town, T023-492050, www.hotel-pagus.hr. This modern, 3-storey hotel is (on the beach) close to the centre of Pag Town and looks out directly onto the beach. It has 117 comfortable rooms, a restaurant with a sunny terrace overlooking Pag Bay, plus a wellness centre offering massage, a sauna, beauty therapies, and an indoor and outdoor pool with jacuzzi. The food is slightly disappointing, so you're best to go B&B, then eat out in the evenings.

€€ **Hotel Boškinac**, Novaljska Polje bb, Novalja, T053-663500, www.boskinac.com. Set amid vineyards, 3 km outside Novalja, this boutique hotel occupies a stone building with 8 rooms and 3 suites, a gourmet restaurant with an open fire and a leafy terrace, and an outdoor pool. The interior features natural materials combined with modern design and vivid colours. They also have their own wine cellars and tasting is available on request.

€ **Camp Straško**, Novalja, T053-661226, www.campingcroatiapag.com. As there are not many good hotels in Novalja, and most people come here to party, camping makes a good option. Overlooking a 2-km stetch of beach, Straško has space for 700 tents. Bungalows are also available.

## Paklenica National Park *p92*

€ **Hotel Rajna**, Tudjmana 105, Starigrad Paklenica, T023-359121, www.hotel-rajna.com. Popular with Croatian and foreign climbers and walkers thanks to its location close to the national park entrance, **Rajna** has 10 guest rooms (most with balconies) and a highly regarded restaurant serving tasty local seafood and meat dishes. They also manage a complex of beautifully restored old stone cottages, called Varoš, and run photo-safari in the park.

## Kornati National Park *p93*

Camping within the park is strictly forbidden. The following Murter-based agencies both have a selection of Robinson Crusoe-type accommodation: simply furnished cottages with gas lighting and water from a well, no cars, no shops and probably no neighbours.
**Kornat Turist**, Hrvatskih vladara 2, T022-435854, www.kornatturist.hr.
**Lori**, Zdrače 2, Betina, T022-435 540, www.touristagency-lori.hr.

## ❼ Restaurants

**Zadar** *p88, map p88*
€€ **Bruschetta**, Mihovila Pavlinovica 12, T023-312915, www.bruschetta.hr. By the sea in the old town, with tables on a sunny waterside terrace, **Bruschetta** serves fresh colourful tasty Mediterranean cuisine. Come here for inexpensive pizza or pasta dishes, or spend a little more and try their succulent steak.

€€ **Dva Ribara**, Blaža Jurjeva 1, T023-213445. Most people come here to eat pizza, but it's also possible to order pasta, risotto, fish and meat dishes. You'll find it in the old town, with a slightly uninspiring modern minimalist interior, and a small terrace for outdoor dining in warm weather.

€€ **Foša**, Ulica kralja Dmitra Zvonimira 2, T023-314421, www.fosa.hr. Close to the Land Gate, just outside the city walls, this is probably the best centrally located fish restaurant. Pasta, risotto, seafood and steak are served on a lovely terrace looking out onto a small harbour.

€€ **Kornat**, Liburnska obala 6, T023-254501, www.restaurant-kornat.com. On the seafront promenade, opposite the ferry port, Kornat was for years considered the best restaurant in town. It has a formal (slightly dated) interior, and serves Croatian dishes spiced up with a dash of Italian flair: look out for gnocchi with *pršut* (prosciutto) and rocket, and tuna steak with green peppercorns.

€€ **Niko**, Obala Kneza Domagoja 9, Puntamika-Borik, T023-337888, www.hotel-niko.hr. Regarded by many as one of the best restaurants in town, **Niko** has been serving Mediterranean cuisine, with an emphasis on seafood, since 1963. There's a lovely waterside terrace and the adjoining hotel has 12 guest rooms (see Where to stay, page 94).

€€ **Pet Bunara**, Trg Pet Bunara bb, T023-224010, www.petbunara.hr. In the old town, close to Trg Pet Bunara, this excellent 'slow food' restaurant takes pride in using fresh seasonal ingredients (mainly organic) to create tasty pizzas, pasta dishes and imaginative salads, plus a limited selection of meat and fish dishes.

**€€ Roko**, Put Dikla 54, Brodarica, on the road from the old town to Borik, T023-331000. This restaurant is owned by a fisherman and serves up spaghetti with shrimps, and lobster, on a summer terrace.

**€ Konoba Stomorica**, Ulica Stomorica 12, T023-315946. In the heart of the old town, this tiny konoba, frequented by local fishermen, serves *girice* (small fried fish) and *pržene lignje* (fried squid), with house wine on tap.

### Cafés and bars

**Forum**, Široka bb, T023-250537. Pleasant café with a terrace overlooking the Roman Forum and the Church of Sveti Donat.

**Kavana Sv Lovre**, Narodni Trg bb, T023-212678. Occupying a former church next to Gradska Straža (City Guardhouse), this is an ideal place to stop while sightseeing in the old town.

**Riva**, Zadarskog Mira 1358, T023-251462. A great spot to have coffee on the seafront promenade in the old town, close to the Forum.

### Island of Pag *p91*

**€€ Boškinac**, Novaljska Polje bb, Novalja, T053-663500, www.boskinac.com. For a true gourmet experience, splash out on dinner at this excellent hotel-restaurant (see Where to stay, page 95), popular with locals and non-residents. Expect a romantic candlelit stone terrace and innovative dishes prepared exclusively from fresh local ingredients – notably seafood, lamb and sheep's cheese. To try a bit of everything opt for one of the *degustacija* (degustation) menus, featuring small portions of either 3, 5 or 7 of the chef's signature dishes. The wines served here come from the Boškinac vineyards. Reservations are recommended.

**€€ Kaštel**, Trg Loza 6, Novalja, T053-661401. On the coast, with a lovely terrace affording views over the bay, **Kaštel** specializes in fresh seafood. Try the fish platter for 2, combining gilthead bream, sea bass, squid and shrimps. Often crowded – reservations recommended.

**€€ Konoba Giardin**, Vanđelje 1, Kolan, T023-698007 www.konobagiardin.com. A classic rustic konoba with heavy wooden tables and benches arranged on a stone patio. Popular with locals, it's a fine choice for traditional Dalmatian specialities such as barbecued meat and fish dishes, as well as lamb or octopus prepared under a peka. You'll find it in the small village of Kolan, approximately midway between Pag Town and Novalja.

**€€ Na Tale**, S Radića 2, Pag Town, T023-611194, Close to the harbour, with outdoor tables and sea views, this small restaurant specializes in barbecued fish and generous portions of Pag lamb, which you might round off with *palačinke* (pancakes). Pizzas are also available.

### Kornati National Park *p93*

The restaurants listed here are all on the west coast of the largest island, Kornat.

**€€ Konoba Opat**, Uvala Opata (Opat Cove), T091-473 2550, www.opat-kornati.com. Jun-Sep. This highly regarded eatery serves delicious seafood specialities such as tuna carpaccio, lobster risotto and John Dory with truffles, plus locally grown olives preserved in sea water, and cake made from carob.

**€€ Restoran Beban**, Uvala Gujka (Gujak Cove), T098-5531588 (mob). Jun-Sep. In a sheltered bay, this is one of the few restaurants in the area to offer *janjetina* (roast lamb), as well as *brodet* (fish stew), seafood and barbecued fish.

**€€ Restoran Darko-Strižnja**, Uvala Strižnja (Strižna Cove), T098-435988 (mob). May-Sep. Fisherman-owner Darko serves up seafood risotto and pasta dishes, *brodet* (fish stew), seafood and barbecued fish, plus fantastic lobster.

## 🌙 Bars and clubs

**Zadar and around** *p88, map p88*
**Arsenal**, Trg Tri Bunar 1, T023-253820, www.arsenalzadar.com. Mon-Thu 0800-2400, Fri-Sat 0800-0200. In the vast 18th-century Venetian arsenal, this arts and entertainment centre includes a restaurant, lounge-bar, a space for exhibitions and concerts, and a wine shop.
**Ledena**, Perivoj Kraljice Jelene Madijevke, T095-9124794, www.ledana.hr. Opened summer 2012, you'll find this lounge-bar in a leafy public garden, close to the entrance into the Old Town. A fine spot for a cocktail on a balmy summer evening.
**Maraschino**, Obala kneza Branimira 6a, T023-224093, www.maraschinobar.hr. Open till late. Named after the sour-cherry liquor that Zadar is famous for, **Maraschino** lies on the coast, with amazing views of the Old Town across the narrow sea channel. Come here for coffee in the sun during the day, or for cocktails, DJ music and a party atmosphere after dark.

**Island of Pag** *p91*
**Novalja**
**Aquarius Club**, Zrče Beach, www.aquarius. hr/zrce. Through summer (Jun-Sep), Zagreb's hottest club moves from the capital to the island of Pag for open-air drinking and dancing by the sea, with regular live concerts given by popular Croatian musicians.
**Kalypso**, Zrče Beach, www.kalypso.com.hr. Palm trees, straw umbrellas, bathing, badminton and beach volleyball by day; music, dancing and cocktails by night.
**Papaya**, Zrče Beach, www.papaya.com.hr. A beach complex with water slides, a bar and a restaurant. Resident and international guest DJs generate a party mood, daily after 2000. It also hosts occasional music festivals.

## 🎭 Festivals

**Zadar** *p88, map p88*
**Mid-Jul to mid-Aug** Music Evenings of St Donat, www.donat-festival.com. Sees a programme of medieval, Renaissance and Baroque music concerts, staged in the Church of St Donat, noted for its exceptional accoustics.
**Late-Aug** Film Forum Zadar, www.film forumzadar.com. Founded in 2010, this 1-week international film festival already has a loyal following.

**Novalja** *p92*
**Jul-Aug** Various multi-day music festivals take place on Zrče beach, with the programme changing each summer.

**Island of Murter** *p93*
**Jul-Aug** Various multi-day music festivals organized at **The Garden**, www.thegarden festival.eu, which has now relocated to Tisno on the island of Murter (previously it was at Petrčane, close to Zadar on the mainland).

## 🛍 Shopping

**Zadar** *p88, map p88*
**Books**
**Algoritam**, City Galleria shopping centre, Murvićka 1, T023-493050. **Algoritam** is the best bookshop for foreign-language publications, including novels, travel guides and maps.

### Clothing
**Mar & Val**, Don Ive Prodana 3, Zadar, T023-213239. Just off Narodni trg (Peoples Square), this boutique stocks clothes, shoes and jewellery by notable Croatian designers such as Ana Maria Ricov.

### Food and drink
**Bibich**, Kraljskog Dalmatina 7, T023-250246. The Bibić family produce their own high-quality wines and herb-flavoured *rakija*, which you can taste and buy here.

**Tržnica**, Old Town. Daily 0700-1400. Open-air fruit and vegetable market in the Old Town.
**Vinoteka Arsenal**, Trg Tri Bunar 1, www.arsenalzadar.com. Inside the arsenal complex, this wine shop stocks wines from Croatia, Australia, Spain, France, Portugal, Chile and Argentina, as well as virgin olive oil from South Dalmatia.

## ☉ What to do

### Zadar and around *p88, map p88*
### Diving
**Blue Bay Diving**, Rupica 17, Stara Novalja, Island of Pag, T091-8871810, www.bluebay diving.com. Instruction and diving trips for all levels, with nearby sites including several wrecks, a cave and abundant underwater life.

### Tour operators
**Surfmania**, Kraljičina plaža, Nin, 22 km from Zadar, T098-9129818, www.surfmania.hr. A windsurfing, kitesurfing and kayaking centre.
**Terra Travel Agency**, Matije Gupca 2a, Zadar, T023-337294, www.terratravel.hr. Excursions from Zadar to Kornati and Paklenica national parks, as well as canoeing and rafting down the River Zrmanja.
**Zadar Sub**, Dubrovačka 20a, Zadar, T023-214848, www.zadarsub.hr. A scuba diving centre based in Zadar, offering instruction and diving trips to the nearby islands.
**Zara Adventure**, Danijela Farlattija 7, Zadar, T023-342368, www.zara-adventure.hr. Caving, trekking, rafting and climbing and rafting in Paklenica National Park and the surrounding area.

## ⊖ Transport

See also Transport in Dubrovnik and South Dalmatian Coast, page 10.

### Zadar *p88, map p88*
### Bus
Frequent buses run to **Zagreb** (3 hrs), **Rijeka** (4 hrs), **Pula** (6 hrs 20 min), **Split** (3½ hrs) and **Dubrovnik** (7½ hrs).

### Train
From Zadar, there are 4 trains daily to **Knin** (2¼ hrs), from where it is possible to take connecting trains to **Zagreb** and **Split**, though this may involve a long wait.

## ☉ Directory

### Zadar *p88, map p88*
**Hospital** Bože Peričića 5, between the old town and the bus station, T023-505505, www.bolnica-zadar.hr. **Pharmacy** Each pharmacy is marked by a glowing green cross. **Ljekarna Donat**, Braće Vranjanina 14, T023-251342, is usually open 24 hrs. If closed, there will be a notice on the door saying which pharmacy to go to.

### Island of Pag *p 91*
**Pharmacy** In Pag Town, Stjepana Radića bb, T023-611043. In Novalja, Dalmatinska 1, T053-661370.

# Contents

Background

# Art and architecture

## Painting and sculpture

The first individual artists to have been recorded in the history of Croatian art were sculptors working in Romanesque style during the 13th century: Master Radovan, who completed the magnificent main portal of Trogir Cathedral, and Andrea Buvina, who carved the well-preserved wooden doors to Split Cathedral. Then, during the 15th century, with the dawn of the Renaissance, some important artists combined the skills of architecture and sculpture, notably Juraj Dalmatinac, who was responsible for the 74 heads cut in stone that make up the freize on the exterior of Šibenik Cathedral, and his pupil Andrea Aleši, who completed the delicately carved baptistry in the same building.

The 15th century also saw the first notable Croatian movement of painters. In the wealthy and culturally advanced city of Dubrovnik, a group of painters inspired by Italian Gothic art and the Byzantine tradition became known as the Dubrovnik School. Unfortunately, few of their works have been preserved – mainly due to the destructive earthquake of 1667 – but Blaž Jurjev Trogiranin (also known as Blasius Pictor) from Trogir and Lovro Dobričević from Kotor (present-day Montenegro) can be singled out. They produced a wealth of icons and ornate polyptychs featuring religious scenes, both for Catholic and Orthodox churches, using rich blues, greens and reds, often against a golden background. Today you can see examples of Trogiranin's work in Korčula Town – a polyptych *Our Lady with Saints* in the Abbey Treasury and a polyptych *Our Lady the Co-redeemer* in the Church of All Saints. Several outstanding pieces by Dobričević are on display in the Dominican Monastery in Dubrovnik.

The country's most noted 19th-century painter is Vlaho Bukovac (1855-1922). Born in Cavtat, he studied in Paris and also spent some time in England, where he executed portraits of various aristocratic families, into which he was received as a friend and guest; his *Potiphar's Wife* was exhibited in the Royal Academy of London. From 1903 to 1922 he was a professor at the Academy of Art in Prague. The house were he was born in Cavtat has been turned into a gallery displaying a collection of his paintings and drawings.

Split's greatest painter is generally acknowledged to be Emanuel Vidović (1870-1953). He studied in Venice then moved back to Split, where he would work outdoors, making colourful sketches, then return to his studio to rework his impressions on large canvasses, often producing dark, hazy paintings with a slightly haunting atmosphere. The Vidović Gallery in Split displays almost 70 of his paintings, donated to the city by his family.

For many people, Croatia's most outstanding 20th-century artist is Edo Murtić (1921-2005). Born in Velika Pisanica near Bjelovar in inland Croatia, he grew up in Zagreb where he also studied art. During the Second World War he designed posters and illustrated books connected to the Partisan liberation movement. After the war he visited New York, where he met American abstract expressionists such as Jackson Pollock, and completed a cycle of paintings called Impressions of America. During the 1960s and 1970s he was one of the masters of European abstract art, painting vast canvasses with mighty bold strokes and daring colours. In the 1980s his works became less abstract, featuring recognizable Mediterranean landscapes. He has paintings in the Tate Gallery in London and MOMA in New York.

Croatia's best-known and most prolific 20th-century sculptor has to be Ivan Meštrovi (1883-1962). Born into a peasant family from the Dalmatian hinterland, he was sent to work with a stonecutter in Split, where he showed considerable skill and was thus sent to study at the Art Academy in Vienna, financed by a Viennese mine owner. Although he did not like his professor, he had great respect for the noted Austrian architect Otto Wagner, who also taught there, and soon became influenced by the Vienna Secession movement. In Vienna he also met Rodin, who inspired him to travel in Italy and France, and then to settle in Paris, where he became internationally renowned. He then spent several years in Rome, mixing with members of the Italian Futurist movement, such as Ungaretti and de Chirico. In 1911 he won first prize at an international exhibition in Rome, where critics hailed him as the best sculptor since the Renaissance.

During the First World War he spent some time in England where he staged a one-man exhibition at London's Victoria and Albert Museum. After the First World War he returned to his homeland, taking a house in Zagreb – which is now open to the public as the Meštrović Atelier – and designing a villa in Split, today the Meštrović Gallery. However, at the beginning of the Second World War he was imprisoned by the fascist Ustaše, and it was only through the intervention of his friends in Italy, including the Pope, that he managed to leave the country. He spent the rest of his life in the USA, but upon his death his body was returned to Croatia where he was buried in the family mausoleum as he had requested. Today he has pieces in stone, bronze and wood on show in the Tate Gallery in London and the Uffizi in Florence. In several Croatian towns you can see bronze statues of important local cultural figures, such as Grgur Ninski and Marko Marulić in Split and Juraj Dalmatinac in Šibenik, which he created as public works. In the US his best-known outdoor piece is *Equestrian Indians* in Grant Park, Chicago.

## Architecture

### Classical

The finest remaining buildings from Roman times can be seen in the cities of Pula and Split. In the former, the oldest significant monument is a first-century BC triumphal arch, known as the Arch of the Sergi. It was built to celebrate the role of three high-ranking military officers from the Sergi family at the Battle of Actium in 31 BC; upon their return home they would have led their triumphant soldiers through the arch into the walled city. Made up of a single arch flanked with slender columns with Corinthian capitals, it is ornamented with base reliefs of dolphins, a sphinx and a griffon, and an eagle struggling with a snake. Originally it would have been topped with statues of the three generals. Italian Renaissance architects Palladio and Michelangelo were obviously suitably impressed by it, as both sketched it on their travels. Close by, the present-day main square was once the forum and, of the principal public buildings that stood here, the first-century AD Temple of Augustus remains intact. Typically designed to be viewed from the front, it is elevated on a high base with steps leading up to an open portico supported by six tall columns. Located outside the former walls, Pula's best-known Roman building is the colossal first-century AD amphitheatre, which was built to host gladiator fights and could accommodate up to 22,000 spectators, making it the sixth largest surviving Roman amphitheatre in the world.

Moving south down the coast, Split grew up within the 25-m-high walls of a unique third-century palace, commissioned by Emperor Diocletian as a retirement residence. Combining the qualities of a Roman garrison and an imperial villa, this vast structure is based on a rectangular ground plan measuring 215 m by 180 m, and contains various individual monuments such as an octagonal mausoleum (now the cathedral) and a classical temple dedicated to Jupiter (now a baptistery). British and French architects and artists first acknowledged its magnificence during the 18th century when many visited it as part of the Grand Tour; it is said to have inspired the Scottish architect Robert Adam in some of his finest neoclassical projects upon his return to the UK.

Some 6 km inland from Split, the archaeological site of Salona was once the largest Roman urban centre in Croatia, with an estimated population of 60,000 in the third century AD. Sadly it was devastated in the seventh century; today only the ruins remain.

During the sixth century the coastal region came under Byzantine rule. Architecturally, the Byzantine Empire is best known for its magnificent Christian basilicas, and the most outstanding example in Croatia is Euphrasius Basilica in Poreč. Built under the rule of Emperor Justinian (AD 483-565), during the same period as Hagia Sophia in Constantinople (present-day Istanbul), this complex comprises a central atrium, with an octagonal baptistery to one side, and opposite it the basilica itself, where the central aisle focuses on a main apse decorated with splendid golden mosaics.

## Pre-Romanesque

The Croats arrived in the region in the seventh century and gradually began taking on the Christian faith. Between the ninth and 11th centuries about 150 small pre-Romanesque churches, often referred to as early Croatian churches, were built, mainly along the coast. Byzantine influence is apparent in their geometric massing, though they tend towards minimum decoration, limited to finely carved stonework ornamented with plait-design motifs reminiscent of Celtic art. The most perfect example is the tiny ninth-century Holy Cross in Nin, based on the plan of a Greek cross, while the largest and most imposing is the monumental ninth-century rotonda St Donat's in Zadar, based on a circular ground plan with three semi-circular apses. You can see an excellent collection of early Croatian church stonework in the Croatian Museum of Archaeological Monuments in Split.

## Romanesque

The 12th century saw the dawn of the Romanesque age, which was marked by imposing cathedrals, generally made up of triple naves with semi-circular apses, and ornate façades featuring blind arches. The most beautiful – the Cathedral of St Anastasia and the Church of St Chrysogonus – are in Zadar, though other notables examples include the Cathedral of Our Lady of the Assumption in Krk Town, the Church of St Mary the Great (which was a cathedral until 1828) in Rab Town, and the portal of the Cathedral of St Lawrence in Trogir, which was carved by the outstanding Dalmatian sculptor Master Radovan in the early 13th century. Unfortunately, Croatia's two most important Romanesque cathedrals were destroyed – the one in Zagreb by the Tartars in 1242, and the one in Dubrovnik by the 1667 earthquake (subsequently rebuilt in later styles).

## Venetian Gothic

When Venice began colonizing the east Adriatic coast, it brought with it the so-called Venetian Gothic style, characterized by the pointed arch and rib vaulting. The style is apparent in 15th- and 16th-century churches and houses in Istria and Dalmatia, such as the finely carved portal of Korčula Cathedral by Bonino from Milan, and the triple pointed-arch windows of the Čipko Palace in Trogir by Andrea Aleši. It is often seen mixed with more severe Renaissance elements, most notably in the work of Juraj Dalmatinac on Šibenik Cathedral (see below), hence the term Gothic-Renaissance.

## Renaissance

The Renaissance, which started in Italy, marked a revival of Roman civilization, not just in art and architecture but in an entire set of values. The movement is normally said to have dawned in Croatia in 1441, when Juraj Dalmatinac, a builder from Zadar who had trained for a short time in Venice, began work on Šibenik Cathedral (although he did not live to see it completed; the later work was carried out by two of his pupils, Nikola Firentinac and Andrija Aleši). Dalmatinac also drew up the urban plan for Pag Town in 1443, and worked on other noted projects, such as the Chapel of St Anastasius in Split Cathedral and Minceta Fortress in Dubrovnik. You can see a 20th-century statue of Dalmatinac, by Ivan Meštrović, in front of Šibenik Cathedral.

The Renaissance continued developing along the coast, in areas that were not under the Turks, until the end of the 16th century. During this period many towns were fortified with defensive walls and towers, the best examples being Dubrovnik, Korčula and Hvar.

Increased wealth, plus the ideals of Renaissance philosophy, lead to the construction of more sophisticated houses, with refined details such as carved doors and window frames, balconies with balustrades, stone washbasins, decorated fireplaces and built-in cupboards. People became interested in the relationship between man and nature; houses were set in gardens with arcaded walkways, fountains and stone benches, the best examples being Tvrdalj in Stari Grad on the island of Hvar and Trsteno Arboretum near Dubrovnik, both from the 16th century.

## Baroque

Regarded as a symbol of Western civilization, and therefore the antithesis of Ottoman culture, the baroque style flourished in northern Croatia during the late 17th and 18th centuries. The Jesuits, who played an important part in reinforcing the Roman Catholic faith in areas threatened by the Turks, were responsible for introducing the grandiose, curvilinear baroque style to the region. As the Turks were gradually pushed out, many buildings were constructed, reconstructed or extended in baroque style.

Today, the best-preserved baroque town centre is in Varaždin; tragically Vukovar, formerly regarded as the finest baroque town in Croatia, was all but devastated during the war of independence during the 1990s. Other notable examples can be found in Osijek (the 18th-century Tvrđa complex) and in Dubrovnik (the Cathedral from 1671 and the Jesuit Church from 1725, both designed by Italian architects during reconstruction following the earthquake of 1667).

## Eclectic

During the 19th century, eclectic design – the revival and reinterpretation of past styles – was popular throughout Europe. In Zagreb, the buildings of Donji Grad, constructed when the region was under Austro-Hungary, mix various elements from classical, Gothic and baroque periods. The most prolific architect in north Croatia at this time was Herman Bolle (1845-1926). Born in Koln, Germany, he participated in the construction of about 140 buildings in Croatia, including Zagreb Cathedral, Mirogoj Cemetery and the Museum of Arts and Crafts, all in Zagreb.

## Vienna Secession

By the close of the 19th century, artists and architects in various parts of Europe were rebelling against the decadence of eclectic buildings and the pomp and formality of older styles, and searching instead for more pure and functional forms. In German-speaking countries this trend was known as Jugendstil, and in France as art nouveau. In 1897 in Vienna, a group of visual artists founded a movement, which became known as the Vienna Secession. The architects involved strove to give simple geometric forms to their buildings, while working in close collaboration with artists, who provided discreet, elegant details such as frescoes and mosaics. The best examples of this style in Croatia, which was still part of the Austro-Hungarian Empire at the time, are Villa Santa Maria, Villa Frappart and Villa Magnolia, all designed by the Austrian architect Carl Seidl and found in Lovran, close to Opatija. In Osijek, Europska Avenue is lined with fine Viennese Secessionist buildings by local architects.

## Modernism

There are very few examples of quality modernist architecture in Croatia, though the ideals of the modern movement were held dear by the Socialist state during the second half of the 20th century. The resulting buildings are primarily high-rise apartment blocks, most of which are light and airy with large balconies, and vast hotel complexes that have sprung up along the coast, which are rather impersonal but functional and comfortable.

# Contents

Footnotes

# Language

Croatian belongs to the South Slavic branch of the Slavic group of languages – a similar language is spoken by Serbs, Montenegrins and Bosnians. Most people working in tourism, as well as the majority of younger Croatians, speak good English, so you won't have much of a problem communicating unless you get off the beaten track. If you do make the effort to learn a few words and phrases, though, your efforts are likely to be rewarded with a smile of appreciation.

## Vowels

| | |
|---|---|
| a | like 'a' in cat |
| e | like 'e' in vet |
| i | like 'i' in sip |
| o | like 'o' in fox |
| u | like 'ou' in soup |

## Consonants

| | |
|---|---|
| c | like 'ts' in bats |
| č | like 'ch' in cheese |
| ć | like 'ch' in future |
| đ | like 'j' in jeans |
| dž | like 'dj' in adjust |
| j | like 'y' in yes |
| lj | like 'ly' in billion |
| nj | like 'ny' in canyon |
| š | like 'sh' in push |

## Numbers

| | |
|---|---|
| 1 | jedan (ye-dan) |
| 2 | dva (dva) |
| 3 | tri (tree) |
| 4 | četri (che-ti-ree) |
| 5 | pet (pet) |
| 6 | šest (shest) |
| 7 | sedam (se-dam) |
| 8 | osam (o-sam) |
| 9 | devet (de-vet) |
| 10 | deset (de-set) |
| 11 | jedanest (ye-'da-na-est) |
| 12 | dvanaest ('dva-na-est) |
| 20 | dvadeset ('dva-de-set) |
| 50 | pedeset (pe-'de'set) |
| 100 | sto (sto) |

## Basics

| | |
|---|---|
| yes | da (da) |
| no | ne (ne) |
| please | molim (mo-lim) |
| thank you | hvala (hva-la) |
| hello | bog (bog) |
| goodbye | dovidjenja (do-vee-'jen-ya) |
| excuse me | oprostite (o-'pro-sti-te) |
| sorry | pardon (par-don) |
| that's OK | u redu je (oo re-doo ye) |
| to | u (oo) |
| from | iz (iz) |
| I (don't) speak Croatian | ja (ne) govorim Hrvatski (Yah ne 'go-vo-rim 'hr-vat-ski) |
| do you speak English? | govorite li vi engleski? (go-vo-ri-te li 'en-gle-ski?) |
| good morning | dobro jutro (do-bro yoo-tro) |
| good afternoon | dobar dan (do-bar dan) |
| good evening | dobro večer (do-bra ve-cher) |
| good night | laku noć (la-koo noch) |
| my name is… | moje ime je… (mo-ye ime ye…) |

## Questions

| | |
|---|---|
| how | kako (ka-ko) |
| when | kada (ka-da) |
| where | gdje (g-dyay) |
| why | zašto (za-shto) |
| what | što (shto) |

## Time

| | |
|---|---|
| morning | *jutro (yoo-tro)* |
| afternoon | *popodne (po-'po-dne)* |
| evening | *večer (ve-cher)* |
| night | *noć (noch)* |
| yesterday | *jučer (yoo-cher)* |
| today | *danas (da-nas)* |
| tomorrow | *sutra (soo-tra)* |
| what time is it? | *koliko je sati?* |
| | *('ko-li-ko ye sa-ti?)* |
| it is… | *točno… (toch-no…)* |
| 0900 | *devet sati (de-vet sa-ti)* |
| midday | *podne (po-dne)* |
| midnight | *ponoć (po-noch)* |

## Days

| | |
|---|---|
| Monday | *Ponedjeljak* |
| | *(Po-'ne-diel-yak)* |
| Tuesday | *Utorak ('Oo-to-rak)* |
| Wednesday | *Srijeda (Sree-ye-da)* |
| Thursday | *Četvrtak (Che-'tvr-tak)* |
| Friday | *Petak (Pe-tak)* |
| Saturday | *Subota ('Soo-bo-ta)* |
| Sunday | *Nedjelja ('Ne-dyel-ya)* |

## Signs and notices

| | |
|---|---|
| Airport | *Aerodrom* |
| Entrance/Exit | *Ulaz/Izlaz* |
| No smoking | *Zabranjeno pušenje* |
| Toilets | *WC* |
| Ladies/Gentlemen | *Ženski/Muški* |

# Index

# Notes

# Notes

# Titles available in the Footprint *Focus* range

| Latin America | UK RRP | US RRP |
|---|---|---|
| Bahia & Salvador | £7.99 | $11.95 |
| Brazilian Amazon | £7.99 | $11.95 |
| Brazilian Pantanal | £6.99 | $9.95 |
| Buenos Aires & Pampas | £7.99 | $11.95 |
| Cartagena & Caribbean Coast | £7.99 | $11.95 |
| Costa Rica | £8.99 | $12.95 |
| Cuzco, La Paz & Lake Titicaca | £8.99 | $12.95 |
| El Salvador | £5.99 | $8.95 |
| Guadalajara & Pacific Coast | £6.99 | $9.95 |
| Guatemala | £8.99 | $12.95 |
| Guyana, Guyane & Suriname | £5.99 | $8.95 |
| Havana | £6.99 | $9.95 |
| Honduras | £7.99 | $11.95 |
| Nicaragua | £7.99 | $11.95 |
| Northeast Argentina & Uruguay | £8.99 | $12.95 |
| Paraguay | £5.99 | $8.95 |
| Quito & Galápagos Islands | £7.99 | $11.95 |
| Recife & Northeast Brazil | £7.99 | $11.95 |
| Rio de Janeiro | £8.99 | $12.95 |
| São Paulo | £5.99 | $8.95 |
| Uruguay | £6.99 | $9.95 |
| Venezuela | £8.99 | $12.95 |
| Yucatán Peninsula | £6.99 | $9.95 |

| Asia | UK RRP | US RRP |
|---|---|---|
| Angkor Wat | £5.99 | $8.95 |
| Bali & Lombok | £8.99 | $12.95 |
| Chennai & Tamil Nadu | £8.99 | $12.95 |
| Chiang Mai & Northern Thailand | £7.99 | $11.95 |
| Goa | £6.99 | $9.95 |
| Gulf of Thailand | £8.99 | $12.95 |
| Hanoi & Northern Vietnam | £8.99 | $12.95 |
| Ho Chi Minh City & Mekong Delta | £7.99 | $11.95 |
| Java | £7.99 | $11.95 |
| Kerala | £7.99 | $11.95 |
| Kolkata & West Bengal | £5.99 | $8.95 |
| Mumbai & Gujarat | £8.99 | $12.95 |

| Africa & Middle East | UK RRP | US RRP |
|---|---|---|
| Beirut | £6.99 | $9.95 |
| Cairo & Nile Delta | £8.99 | $12.95 |
| Damascus | £5.99 | $8.95 |
| Durban & KwaZulu Natal | £8.99 | $12.95 |
| Fès & Northern Morocco | £8.99 | $12.95 |
| Jerusalem | £8.99 | $12.95 |
| Johannesburg & Kruger National Park | £7.99 | $11.95 |
| Kenya's Beaches | £8.99 | $12.95 |
| Kilimanjaro & Northern Tanzania | £8.99 | $12.95 |
| Luxor to Aswan | £8.99 | $12.95 |
| Nairobi & Rift Valley | £7.99 | $11.95 |
| Red Sea & Sinai | £7.99 | $11.95 |
| Zanzibar & Pemba | £7.99 | $11.95 |

| Europe | UK RRP | US RRP |
|---|---|---|
| Bilbao & Basque Region | £6.99 | $9.95 |
| Brittany West Coast | £7.99 | $11.95 |
| Cádiz & Costa de la Luz | £6.99 | $9.95 |
| Granada & Sierra Nevada | £6.99 | $9.95 |
| Languedoc: Carcassonne to Montpellier | £7.99 | $11.95 |
| Málaga | £5.99 | $8.95 |
| Marseille & Western Provence | £7.99 | $11.95 |
| Orkney & Shetland Islands | £5.99 | $8.95 |
| Santander & Picos de Europa | £7.99 | $11.95 |
| Sardinia: Alghero & the North | £7.99 | $11.95 |
| Sardinia: Cagliari & the South | £7.99 | $11.95 |
| Seville | £5.99 | $8.95 |
| Sicily: Palermo & the Northwest | £7.99 | $11.95 |
| Sicily: Catania & the Southeast | £7.99 | $11.95 |
| Siena & Southern Tuscany | £7.99 | $11.95 |
| Sorrento, Capri & Amalfi Coast | £6.99 | $9.95 |
| Skye & Outer Hebrides | £6.99 | $9.95 |
| Verona & Lake Garda | £7.99 | $11.95 |

| North America | UK RRP | US RRP |
|---|---|---|
| Vancouver & Rockies | £8.99 | $12.95 |

| Australasia | UK RRP | US RRP |
|---|---|---|
| Brisbane & Queensland | £8.99 | $12.95 |
| Perth | £7.99 | $11.95 |

For the latest books, e-books and a wealth of travel information, visit us at: www.footprinttravelguides.com.

Join us on facebook for the latest travel news, product releases, offers and amazing competitions: www.facebook.com/footprintbooks.